CANINE HIP DYSPLASIA
and other
orthopedic problems

Canine Hip Dysplasia
and Other Orthopedic Problems

Fred L. Lanting

with contributions by
Dr. Wayne H. Riser and Dr. Sten-Erik Olsson

1981
Alpine Publications, Inc.
1901 South Garfield, Loveland, Colorado

Library of Congress Cataloging in Publication Data

Lanting, Fred L   1936-
  Canine hip dysplasia and other orthopedic problems.

  Bibliography: p.
  Includes index.
    1.   Canine hip dysplasia.   3.   Veterinary orthope-
dics.   3.   Dogs—Anatomy.   4.   Dogs—Diseases.
  I.   Title.
SF992.H56L36   636.7'0897581   79-54235
ISBN 0-931866-06-5

International Standard Book Number 0-931866-06-5
Library of Congress Catalog Card Number 79-54235

Printed in the United States of America.

To my wife, Jeanne

Who, after all those years of answering
 the phone and letters,
scooping up and hosing down the kennels,
stuffing pills down unwilling little throats,
puppy-sitting while the pro handler in the family
 took a van full of other people's dogs to shows,
being gradually converted from carpet to tile as the ideal flooring,
picking up and selling dog food and other items,
sleeping on a cot next to the whelping box,
and repeatedly sorting through files, photographs,
 contracts, and other records for forgotten data,
has now begun to realize how it could be
 that a man could bring forth a child,
a book, with the travails of labor some think
 only a woman understands.

vi

Contents

Foreword

By writing this book on canine hip dysplasia, the author and contributors, in my opinion, have satisfied a long-standing need for a comprehensive, up-to-date source of information concerning this disease which affects so many dog breeds.

I became intimately involved with canine hip dysplasia in the late 1960's. As a breeder of German Shepherd Dogs, and having experienced the emotional upset of having dysplastic animals, I decided to devote my energies to doing anything possible to alleviate, or hopefully eliminate, this disease.

Working with the Eye Dog Foundation and later with International Guiding Eyes, a protocol was developed which ultimately lowered the incidence of canine hip dysplasia in these kennels of German Shepherd Dogs to less than ten percent.

This was accomplished by using only absolutely radiographically normal parents based at twenty-four months of age; plus palpating, progeny testing, screening, and eliminating the undesirable offspring. I used these same procedures with other kennels and breeds with the same degree of success.

A message to the breeders who are desireous of working toward reducing the incidence of canine hip dysplasia in their line. By reading this book you can see that much has been written and theorized about HD. However, in the final analysis, using absolutely radiographically normal OFA parents and progeny testing, in my opinion, is the only way this disease entity can be reduced.

I hope that some day, in the not too distant future, a positive identification program will be implemented, thereby insuring that there be no question as to the identity of the animal being radiographed. In this area the SV is ahead of us in the USA. I have proposed this to the OFA, but as to date, I have not been convincing enough. Perhaps some of you readers may succeed toward this end.

Joseph F. Giardina, D.V.M.
Tarzana, California

x

Acknowledgments

No man is an island, and I am deeply grateful to those who have surrounded me with support and encouragement, as well as technical data and the benefit of their personal experience.

There are obvious contributions by Dr. Wayne Riser and Dr. Sten-Erik Olsson, who each have given a chapter to this book, and by Dr. Richard Huff, whose testimonial and report of years of work on palpation is presented as an appendix. Dr. Giardina's comments and contribution are also appreciated.

But there are so many others who have given their time and talents to enrich my own knowledge and experience over the years: Dr. Kasstrom has provided many photographs, as have Dr. Cardinet, Dr. Grondalen, Dr. Huff, Dr. Krook, Dr. Olsson, Dr. Pharr, and others. The international nature of the help is apparent in these names. Radiographs have been contributed by Dr. Bartels, Dr. Burt, and Dr. Grondalen, and others have been obtained through the patience and assistance of my local private practitioner, Dr. Charles Young. In addition, numerous breeders and veterinarians have given me case histories and radiographs to study.

A good deal of time has been spent with and by Dr. John Bardens, Dr. Huff, Dr. Riser, and Dr. Young. Other than professional services, this time was donated in the interest of friendship and education. Reprint permission from the *American Kennel Gazette*, Gaines, and the F.C.I. have greatly helped add depth to this work.

I appreciate the advice, the time, the materials, and the friendships developed through the years. They have made this erstwhile island feel like a continent.

Preface

When I asked a well-known veterinarian what motivated him to devote so much effort to the study of hip dysplasia, besides the desire to search out knowledge that the study of science encourages, he told me of the large number of personal pets which at one year of age or more could barely walk, though many were from supposedly normal parents. He saw the broken hearts and spirits of clients who were faced with telling their children that their beloved dogs had to be destroyed, and he determined to take a fresh, hard look at "HD" and find some ways to get it under control. Every veterinarian learns early in his schooling that one of his prime functions is to alleviate the suffering in animals. The same love for "all creatures great and small" that veterinarians share with most animal fanciers has prompted much work and stimulated a lot of thought in the area of this disease.

Although I had had dogs all my life, with our first purebred litter whelped in 1946 and the acquisition of our first German Shepherd Dog in 1948, it was not until 1966 that circumstances allowed me to start breeding and handling professionally at dog shows. It was about this time (1966) that the Orthopedic Foundation for Animals (OFA) book by Riser and Miller was published.[71]* One of my early observations in handling was the large number of dogs which were afflicted with hip dysplasia; my desire to prevent that pain in my own breeding program, coupled with my education and training in science, led to increasing research into the cause and control of canine hip dysplasia.

Have you ever had a dog which was reluctant to run and play with others when about six to nine months of age? One which perhaps indicated, if not pain and limping, at least some discom-

---

***Editor's note:** these numbers appearing throughout the text refer to references listed by number at the end of the book.

fort and restricted movement especially in the rear? Hip dysplasia affects dogs in different degrees . . . the severity is one factor, and the amount of pain any particular dog can stand is another.

Since I was both a breeder and a professional dog-show handler in the late 1960's and early-to-mid 1970's, innumerable dogs were brought to me for inspection. I was able to do what Dr. Richard Huff calls a "motion and gait analysis" on each of these, advising their owners as to the dogs' suitability for the show ring, where fluid, ground-covering gait is extremely important. Quite a few of these dogs had a short stride even though the rear angulation ("bend of stifle") would have indicated otherwise. Typically, the worst cases limped, and sometimes it was difficult to tell which limb was the most favored. I suspect these dogs were equally uncomfortable in each hip.

A great number of these dogs were radiographed ("X-rayed") as a result of my comments, and the owners and veterinarians were kind enough to share the results with me. More and more case histories and radiographs came to me as my magazine articles were published and as my puppies grew and their new owners assisted with follow-up information. It quickly became apparent to me that hip dysplasia was not only a painful situation for the dog, but an emotional and economic problem to the owner and breeder as well.

Thanks to the reasonable services of Dr. Huff in palpating somewhere in excess of a hundred of our puppies, using the method developed by Dr. John Bardens, I was fortunate to gain much experience and data in the area of hip dysplasia. One day Mrs. V.__ came to me and asked me what was wrong with her dog. The following case history illustrates a fairly typical story of HD. This one had a happy ending:

The dog was dragging its hindquarters and exhibiting other symptoms (see Chapters 1 and 4) which made me believe that it likely had Grade 4 dysplasia. I recommended X-ray diagnosis which confirmed my suspicions, and her veterinarian despaired of hope and suggested euthanasia. Like most other pet owners, Mrs. V.__ didn't want that solution. I told her an option would be to take the dog to Ohio State University Veterinary School for a fairly new surgical approach to alleviation of pain. Subsequently the dog had a bilateral pectineal myotomy (see Chapter 9).

Dr. Bardens, one of the pioneers in that field of surgery, takes out a large section of the pectineus muscle, thus eliminating the tension which pulls the leg bone out of the hip socket. Dr. Hohn had been doing a resection at the far end and cutting the adductor muscles as well. His colleague at Ohio State, Dr. Rudy, made his incisions high, near the pelvis. Whichever method is used, they result in cessation of pain and return of useful perambulation. While the following testimonial was written three and a half years after the treatment, other case histories show that dogs are normally active for many more years after such an operation. Here is Mrs. V.__'s letter:

"During December of 1971, we noticed our six month old German Shepherd Dog, Prince, was having difficulty walking and sitting. His hind legs crossed when he walked and one of his hips looked higher than the other when he was standing. After having him examined by Dr. G. in Cleveland, we met with Dr. Rudy at Ohio State and were again advised to have Prince put to sleep. However, if we decided against this course of action, he would perform an operation that would not *cure* Prince of the hip dysplasia but that it would definitely relieve him of the discomfort he was enduring. The operation was performed later that afternoon.

"Almost two weeks later when we picked up Prince, . . . he was very cheerful and pleased to see us, despite the fact that he was extremely skinny from not eating and he was pretty weak from lack of exercise. Before our leaving, Dr. Rudy met with us to explain what he had done and emphasized that Prince would need plenty of exercise to get his muscles stretched and back to normal. This was no problem, for Prince is a very active dog, extremely playful and very strong. He loves to be outdoors and enjoys running. He doesn't know what it means to lie down and rest; he is constantly in motion.

"During the spring and summer of 1972 he ran a mud path in the backyard (which was once very thick grass) as he chased birds *all* day. He jumps all the time, runs down stairs jumping the last five or six without any fear or discomfort when he reaches the bottom, and he hurdles daily a three-foot gate which was put between the living room and dining room . . . when the mailman comes every day. To see him, no one would ever suspect he had "bad" hips."

Yes, hip dysplasia can be a very painful disease, to both the dog and the owner. But there is hope for the individual. And there are measures you can take to benefit your chosen breed also. Why gamble when you can read this book and know what to do? To paraphrase an old card player's phrase, "read it and reap" . . . reap the benefit of the experience of many others and you won't have so much to learn the hard way.

Fred L. Lanting
March 1980

Introduction

Hip dysplasia is a complex disease commonly occurring in most domesticated species including man, and controlled to a great degree in the wild by the process known as natural selection. Its nature has been described as biochemical in that it is basically controlled by those chemical transmitters of inheritance called genes, and biomechanical in that it is influenced strongly by physical stresses. It is usually characterized by both an unstable hip joint and secondary degenerative joint disease.[66]* A more complete interpretation of this brief definition will be developed as the text proceeds, but an initial conceptualization might be the lateral subluxation** of the top of the thigh bone (femur) from the socket in the hip bone (pelvis). Normally, the ball-shaped head of the femur fits tightly into the socket (acetabulum). In many cases it doesn't, and therein lies a source of endless tears, arguments, controversy, and conflict, as well as some pain and crippling on the *dog's* part.

A long-time student of dysplasia, the late Dr. Gerry Schnelle, gave credit to Hippocrates for reporting hip dysplasia initially in 300 B.C.[77] Dr. Schnelle, who first published an account of canine hip dysplasia in the mid-thirties,[81,82] noted that hip dysplasia has been observed in humans and other mammals, which he said suggests something other than a purely genetic cause. While many if not most individuals recover from the acute phase on their own,[79] the dog with pain deserves help and its owner deserves information and advice on control of hip dysplasia. This, in part, is the aim of this book.

---

*Editor's note:** these numbers appearing throughout the text refer to references listed by number at the end of the book.
**The condition in which the femur only loosely fits into the socket.

Hip dysplasia is not an all-or-none phenomenon. Even in hips rated "normal" differences can be observed. At birth, the canine hip joint is normal;[54, 70] intrauterine stresses are not sufficient to deform the hip. In the human, however, and especially in the case of the firstborn, tightness of the uterus often puts abnormal stresses on relatively longer legs and consequently on the soft tissues of the hip. So it is not uncommon for some children to be born with unstable hip joints.

In the canine, the most critical period in the development of the hip joint is from birth to two months of age. Bones have not

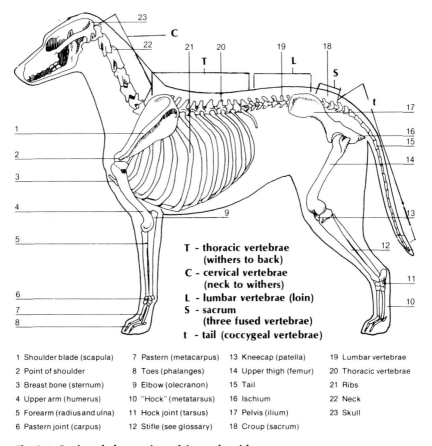

T - thoracic vertebrae
   (withers to back)
C - cervical vertebrae
   (neck to withers)
L - lumbar vertebrae (loin)
S - sacrum
   (three fused vertebrae)
t - tail (coccygeal vertebrae)

1 Shoulder blade (scapula)	7 Pastern (metacarpus)	13 Kneecap (patella)	19 Lumbar vertebrae
2 Point of shoulder	8 Toes (phalanges)	14 Upper thigh (femur)	20 Thoracic vertebrae
3 Breast bone (sternum)	9 Elbow (olecranon)	15 Tail	21 Ribs
4 Upper arm (humerus)	10 "Hock" (metatarsus)	16 Ischium	22 Neck
5 Forearm (radius and ulna)	11 Hock joint (tarsus)	17 Pelvis (ilium)	23 Skull
6 Pastern joint (carpus)	12 Stifle (see glossary)	18 Croup (sacrum)	

Fig. I-1. Canine skeleton viewed from the side.

fully formed from cartilage, the muscles and nerves are not fully developed, and the soft, plastic tissues of the genetically defective hip can be strained beyond their elastic limit* if the stresses exceed the strength of the hip. Once the acetabulum and the femoral head have lost congruity, bone formation will be abnormal.

---

*That point on a stress-strain curve beyond which the material being tested does not return to its original size and shape.

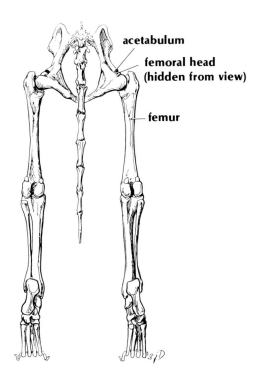

Fig. I-2. View from the rear (caudal view).

If one looks at the nature of hip dysplasia from the points of view of both an engineer and a veterinarian, one can visualize two premises: that hip dysplasia occurs when instability and incongruity develop in the young animal, and that the disease can be prevented or retarded in the individual if congruity can be maintained until bone formation is sufficiently complete and surrounding muscles sufficiently strong to prevent subluxation. Hip dysplasia has been experimentally prevented by confining young pups to small cages in which the dogs had to sit on their haunches most of the time, with hind legs flexed.[71] This is obviously not a satisfactory method of rearing a dog to become a well-adjusted member of one's family. Human babies are put into splints or special diapers that abduct (spread) the legs and flex them as well, thus seating the femoral head more deeply into the acetabulum than it would be otherwise, until further development and strengthening of the joint takes place.

In this work, practical methods of maintaining congruity during maturation are proposed for controlling the disease in the individual dog, and methods of control through breeding are suggested. Major theories as well as some minor but more recent ones on the cause of canine hip dysplasia are outlined and not so much analyzed as discussed, with an attempt to balance impartiality with accuracy and experience.

Stress on the hip joints of the dog begins when the pup forces itself to the dam's teats, and later when it walks. If that stress pulls the joint apart beyond normal clearance, the effect may be so mild as to be hardly distinguishable, or so severe that it becomes difficult to call it a joint at all. They may show up early or late, and appear to be correlated with the severity of and exposure to the architectural imbalance.[74]

Glossary

Abduct   To move away from (each other).

Acetabulum   That part of the pelvis which acts as a socket for the head of the femur.

Acute   Type of or stage of a disease characterized by a sudden onset or change, sharp or severe pain, or sensitive nature.

Adduct   To move toward (each other).

Allele   One of a pair of genes. See Homozygous & Heterozygous.

Arthritis   Inflammation (-itis) of a joint (arthr-).

Bunny-hopping   Advancing and extending both hind legs together, so the weight at the rear of the dog is not carried by only one of those limbs.

Calcitonin   A hormone secreted by the thyroid, which lowers calcium level in the blood by inhibiting bone resorption. It also increases urinary excretion of phosphate.

Cartilage   White, nearly opaque connective tissue devoid of capillaries. Gristle.

Chronic   Of long duration; often follows an acute stage or condition.

Clinical   Observable in the living patient, obvious, frank. Clinical signs are called symptoms.

Condyles   The "knobs" on the ends of certain bones.

Congenital   With (con-) birth (-geni-). In this work, referring to the fact HD is present at or before birth, even though presently not detectable until later. The word is also variously used to mean hereditary (in the genes) or a "birth defect" occurring as the result of some trauma in the uterus or during birth.

Congruity   Fitting together, as a square peg in a square hole, usually without much space left over.

Connective tissue   Usually refers to such non-vascular tissues as the periosteum, ligaments, and fascia (fibrous tissue between and forming the sheaths of muscles). In larger usage, any tissues supporting the essential or specialized part of an organ. Includes adipose, areolar, cartilaginous, lymphatic, and other tissues.

Cow-hocks   Improper stance in dogs. Viewed from the rear, the hocks (heels) are closer together than are other parts of the rear legs.

Coxofemoral   The area where hip or pelvis (coxa) and thigh (femur) meet.

Creep   A slow deformation or slide produced by a steady or repeated force (but not an impact). Usually produces microfractures in the bones subjected to such force. Cartilage drift is a specific example of creep.

Diagnosis   Determination of the identity or nature of a disease.

Distal   Further from the torso.

Dysplasia   Bad form—can refer to deformed cells or larger structures. Most often used to refer to hip joints.

Eburnation   Bone losing its protective cartilaginous covering and allowing bone to abrade against bone.

Elastic limit   Point at which a material (in this work, bone or cartilage) will not return to the shape and dimensions it had before stresses were applied.

Etiology   The study of the causes of disease. Pathogenesis is the study of the course or mode of operation, but these two words are often used interchangeably.

Euthanasia   Killing an animal calmly, easily, without pain; often used to prevent further pain in a patient with a terminal and/or painful disease or condition.

Exostoses   Bony growths or deposits, usually on the edge or surface of a bone at or near a joint. May have chemical (nutrition, hormone, etc.) or physical (stress, eburnation) causes.

Fatigue   The weakening of a material or an organ, usually non-reversible, often leading to failure after repeated application of stresses.

Femur   Thigh bone, consisting of ball-shaped head, neck, shaft, and condyles at the bottom.

Fossa   Socket or depression; in this work, the deeper "cup" part of the acetabulum.

Genotype   The actual genetic make-up of a dog, in this case, which it can pass along to offspring. See Phenotype & Heterozygous.

Growth plate   Line of cells between the end of a bone and its major portion, usually the shaft; the length of the bone is increased by cartilage cells being ossified and similar changes in this region.

Hemorrhage   Internal bleeding.

Heterozygous   One member of a gene pair is chemically different than the other. Hence, the animal can pass a certain characteristic (determined by one gene) to one offspring through a sperm or egg cell, and a different characteristic to another (See Chapter 11).

Histology   The study of cells, tissues, and organs. Usually utilizes dissection, cross-section, examination of bone apart from other tissues, and microscopic examination.

Hock   1) The heel, that joint where tibia and fibula of lower rear leg meet the tarsal bones.
2) In some breed standards, often used to refer to the tarsus itself, that part of the rear foot between the actual hock joint and the pad.

Homozygous   Both members of a pair of genes which the animal passes to its progeny are the same. It cannot transmit any other specific characteristic than what it has to give.

Hormone   A chemical produced by a gland or organ or part of an organ, having a regulatory effect on other organs. For example, the hormone class called "estrogens" may affect the way joints are shaped, either before or after birth.

Lateral   Toward the outside of center.

Laxity   Abnormal looseness, lack of tight fit in the coxo-femoral joint.

Lesion   Structural or functional evidence of a disease.

Ligament   Connective tissue surrounding and supporting joints; connective tissue within a joint, such as the "round" or teres ligament.

Luxation   A condition in which one structure is separated from another structure, as the head of the femur completely out of the hip socket.

Medial   Toward the center.

Morphology   The study of form and structure which encompasses anatomy, histology, and cytology (cells). The combining form "morph" refers to death or a narcotic simulation of death, and morphologic study usually requires euthanasia or the cutting of dead bodies or parts thereof.

Myopathy   Disease (pathy) of a muscle (myo-).

Orthopedics   Branch of science or surgery dealing with diseases or deformities of the bones, joints, and allied tissues.

Osteophytes   Bony outgrowths; abnormal protuberances on a bone or joint.

Palpation   Feeling, generally with the hands. In this book it usually refers to the Bardens technique of detecting laxity in two-month old puppies' hips.

Parathormone   (Parathyroid hormone) another glandular secretion affecting calcium level in the circulatory system (*See* Calcitonin and Chapter 10).

Patella   The "knee cap" at the stifle.

Pathology   The study of (-logy) a disease (path-).

Pelvis   That collection of fused bones which connect the thigh bones with the "backbone" (*See* drawing on p. 71).

Periosteum   The white fibrous membrane which is the covering of bones except at their articulating surfaces or where ligaments and tendons are attached, in which case cartilage is the covering tissue.

Phenotype   The "outward" appearance, including radiographic and morphologic information (*See* Genotype and Chapter 13).

Plastic   Deformable; able to be shaped or distorted.

Progeny   Offspring of and by either sex. At one time the word "get" referred to the progeny only of a male, but the distinction is now obsolescent. "Produce," as a noun and with the first syllable accented, is also an archaic synonym for "progeny."

Progeny Testing   In this work, a means of "educated guessing" at a dog's genetic make-up, or relative number of genes for good or bad hips, by examining its offspring for the signs of HD.

Prognosis   Prediction of the course or outcome of a disease.

Proximal   Close to the body or torso.

Radiograph   Picture made by X-rays passing through various tissues and exposing a photographic film. Shadows cast by bones and other "radiopaque" articles show up clearer on the negative-image film; other parts of the film are more exposed and appear darker. When a print is made of the radiograph, the under-exposed, clear portions appear white.

Remodelling   Bone and joint changes or abnormalities resulting from stresses applied to the "wrong" portions. Radiographic, histologic, or morphologic evidence of hip dysplasia's secondary degenerative action.

Scurvy   Symptoms caused by Vitamin C deficiency.

Stifle   1) The knee joint and surrounding tissues on the rear leg (see Fig. I-1).
2) The sweep of the rear leg from mid-thigh to just before the hock. Breed standards refer to stifles being straight, moderate, and well-bent.

Strain   The reaction to stress (forces), as in a strained ligament or muscle. Often some damage occurs which may not be apparent until repeated stresses are applied.

Stress   The force exerted on an object.

Sub-clinical   Not observable by usual means; symptoms may be deduced or discovered by unusual methods of inquiry and may not be the classical obvious signs.

Subluxation   A synonym for hip dysplasia, referring to the joint looseness in which the head of the femur is not in close congruity to the hip socket (acetabulum), but neither is it completely out of that socket.

Tendon   Connective tissue forming the transition from muscle to periosteum and bone.

Tissue   A collection of cells of the same type. An organ consists of one or more types of tissues performing one function.

Thorax   The upper part of the torso; the chest, from neck to abdomen.

Trauma   Injury, usually with a physical or mechanical cause.

Vascular   Having to do with veins, arteries, and capillaries.

X-rays   Energy radiation similar to light but not visible to human sight. Waves in this frequency and wavelength range pass easily through most substances such as flesh, but some are filtered or absorbed as they pass through more dense material. Thus radiation can produce a shadow "picture" (-graph) on a previously unexposed photographic film and thus give the radiologist insight into the outlines and structure of bones and other organs and articles.

SECTION I
Diagnosis, Occurrence, and Cause

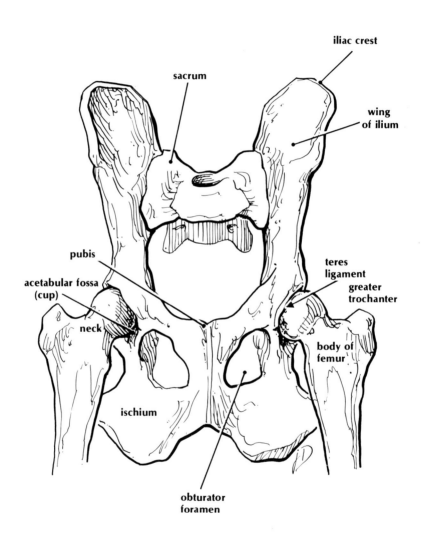

Figure 1-1. Pelvis and hip joints in traditional x-ray position

Chapter 1
Diagnosis

Clinical Signs*

Often referred to as HD, hip dysplasia in the canine can sometimes be identified through a study of the individual dog in motion, although the only accurate diagnosis is made by reading a pelvic radiograph ("X-ray picture"). Most breeds have a wide spectrum of tactile sensitivity or threshold of pain, so that one dog with a mild form of hip dysplasia may be very uncomfortable much of the time, while another with more severe dysplasia may exhibit no pain or limping whatsoever. The distinction between clinically and radiographically determined hip dysplasia is important to breeder, veterinarian, and pet owner alike.

Generally, but not always, dogs with the worst "X-rays" will have the most severely affected gait. Dogs developing hip dysplasia will often exhibit a crippling lameness by five to eight months of age. Lesser degrees of severity will be manifested in an unwillingness to stay out in cold weather, difficulty in rising on the hind legs or climbing stairs, dragging the rear toenails, or a lack of stamina in roadwork or play. One day the dog might show some or all of these signs, while on other days perhaps show none.

Sometimes dysplasia in the young dog will be discovered suddenly when it becomes acutely lame, whether following a trauma such as slipping on ice or wet grass, or without an observed cause. The pup's weight on an unstable joint, magnified by the forces of twisting and turning during play, can pull a loose, incompletely-formed joint apart and produce pain. Some of the soft tissues and the rim of the acetabulum may tear or fracture, resulting in obvious gait changes even after the acute episode subsides.

---

*Clinical signs are symptoms observed in the living dog outside of the laboratory, X-ray room, or surgeon's table.

A dog with more than the most mild form of hip dysplasia may take shorter steps than a dog with normal or near-normal hips. It may also "toe-in" at the rear, with stifles (knees) held closely together. But this in itself is not a sure sign; some dogs have inherited a characteristic walk with rear toes pointing inward just a little, although their hips may be normal.

"Cow-hocks" and rolling gait are mentioned as signs of dysplasia, but it must be remembered that such conditions are seen in normal-hip dogs as well, possibly due to loose ligaments, excessive bone length or angulation, and/or rotated bones. A couple of breed standards actually call for a rolling gait!

The more signs that appear together, the more suspicious it becomes. Clinical signs in pups may include "bunny hopping" and sitting on one haunch, especially when other pups of the same age have outgrown those traits. When it appears in older pups or mature dogs of one or two years of age, hip dysplasia may be evidenced by difficulty in getting up quickly or an apparent discomfort when standing on all fours. Some dogs will lean forward with head lowered in an attempt to shift some weight forward and off the rear quarters. Hind legs may cross over when trotting, as seen fairly easily from the rear. One sign by itself should not lead to any conclusion.

Adult dogs may have intermittent lameness which develops into chronic lameness after four years of age. This is caused by secondary degenerative joint disease (arthritis), the scene having been set much earlier in life. Some dogs will not be able to stand much pressure laterally or downward on the hindquarters; at dog shows some judges will test a dog's resistance to pressure, though a dog which has not been trained to stand for examination, or one which is in early obedience training may also sit when pushed on the sacrum.* A good judge, it is hoped, can tell the difference.

Radiographic Signs

A good radiograph, taken of a properly positioned dog, will show how deeply set within the acetabulum the femoral head is and how much, if any, deviation from normal there is in the bony structures of the joint. Radiography gives the only definitive determination of hip dysplasia in the living animal, and its use has been increasing in recent years. Breeders and others are forsaking the old head-in-the-sand attitude[78] and looking for every tool they can use in the fight against hip dysplasia.

---

*The top of the pelvis where spine ends and tail begins; croup.

Chapter 2
The Orthopedic Foundation
For Animals
and the Radiograph

History of the OFA

Conferences and informal meetings were held in the 1950's and 60's, and in February of 1959 the National Institute of Health (NIH) sponsored one on Comparative Pathology of Arthritis and Rheumatism, resulting in part in a financial grant to study canine hip dysplasia. Much of the information we have today came directly or indirectly from these efforts.

In 1961 the American Veterinary Medicine Association (AVMA) held a special session with a dozen veterinarians and established techniques and standards for producing and interpreting radiographs. The meeting was reported in the AVMA Journal.[88] Later, the American College of Veterinary Radiology was founded and carried out these findings.

Because of the great variations in radiographic opinions prior to that meeting, the Golden Retriever Club of America set up a registry for diagnosis of pelvic radiographs, naming Mrs. Vern Bower as chairman. She sent all submitted films to three veterinarians and a diagnosis of normal or dysplastic was made. A relatively small number of films (about 200) was processed, but the registry formed the basis for the Orthopedic Foundation for Animals in the mid sixties.

The first breed clubs to give moral and financial support were the Golden Retriever Club and the German Shepherd Dog Club of America. The latter donated $5,000 for the printing of a book, the contents of which were a result of discoveries by its author, Dr. Riser, with an NIH grant.[71] Other notables joining the movement early were Labrador Retriever fancier and philanthropist John Olin, Dr. George Gardner, writer, dog fancier Harry Miller, Dr. Frank Booth, an AKC judge and former secretary of the American Animal Hospital Association, Dr. Julius Fishler, and Dr. W. H. Rhodes.

The OFA set up its initial office at the School of Veterinary Medicine, University of Pennsylvania, at Philadelphia on August 1, 1966, with Dr. Wayne Riser as director. Its goals were to:

1. Collate and disseminate information concerning orthopedic diseases of animals;
2. Encourage and establish control programs to lower the incidence of orthopedic diseases;
3. Promote research in orthopedic diseases; and
4. Receive and distribute grants to carry out such objectives.

In a couple of years the project outgrew its space at the University of Pennsylvania and the College of Veterinary Medicine at the University of Missouri agreed to furnish facilities, with Dr. Stanley Larsen assuming the post of project director.[17] Later, John Olin donated a building that became the OFA's headquarters. Today the OFA is self-supporting, with the exception of receiving utilities from the University.[68]

Interpretation

Standards for evaluating radiographs (one of the most important activities of OFA radiologists) are closely adhered to by a group of board-certified veterinary radiologists, members of the American College of Veterinary Radiology. Each film is read and diagnosed by three different radiologists in various parts of the country, and a consensus report is issued. Evaluations result in a submitted radiograph being categorized as Normal (Excellent, Good, or Fair) or Dysplastic (Mild, Moderate, or Severe); suspicious films are given an additional classification of Borderline, and another reading of a radiograph taken when the dog is older is suggested. Certification of a film is given if the hips are within the normal range after the dog is two years of age. When the radiograph is designated as normal, the dog receives an OFA certification or registration number.

Examples of normal and dysplastic hip radiographs appear in this work and in many of the publications listed in the references. An owner wishing to obtain an OFA evaluation of his dog, whatever its age, may do so by arranging it with a veterinarian. The film would be mailed to OFA, c/o University of Missouri, Columbia, MO 65211. If you intend to breed your dog, let your veterinarian know ahead of time that you might want a radiograph sent to the OFA. This will enable him to prepare the film according to OFA guidelines, and will leave no doubt in his mind as to what your concern is and the reason for radiographing.

What is seen on the radiograph? Since hip dysplasia has been described as "a deformity of the coxofemoral joint or joints which may be characterized radiographically by a shallow acetabulum, flattening of the femoral head, coxofemoral subluxation, or secondary degenerative joint disease,"[17] one may logically expect to see one or several of these characteristics, although not necessarily in all cases can one determine hip dysplasia upon viewing a radiograph.[33] There are age and breed variables, the positioning of the dog and the proper exposure of the film may vary slightly, and the standard film evaluates only the phenotype of the dog at the time of radiography, not its genotype. That is, it does not give a clue as to whether that dog carries the propensity for dysplasia, or in what degree if it is not seen on the film, but only whether that animal has radiographic evidence itself. Regardless of any limitations, radiography remains the best diagnostic tool we have, especially in the adult dog.

At What Age to Radiograph?

The dog owner can get an evaluation from OFA at any age, though no certification is given until the dog is two years old. At one time, dogs were certified at 12 months. The age requirement was changed because hips sometimes became remodelled and radiographically dysplastic as the dog grew another year or so. The old categories of Normal, Near-normal, and Dysplastic were also enlarged and clarified. Readings at six months or so by experienced radiologists are of great help in getting information on which to partly base one's decisions in culling litters.

As of January 1, 1974, certification could only be given if the dog were two years or older. In one study,[36] standard radiographs taken at one year revealed only about 69 percent of the German Shepherd Dogs and 62 percent of the Vizslas that would eventually show hip dysplasia, while at two years 92-95 percent of the dysplastic dogs were detected.

TABLE I. PERCENT DETECTED AS DYSPLASTIC AT GIVEN AGE IN MONTHS

BREED	AGE: 6 mo.	12 mo.	18 mo.	24 mo.	36 mo.
German Shepherd Dog	15.8	68.9	82.7	95.4	97.5
Vizsla	32.4	62.5	72.5	92.5	97.5

*Since there is no doubt that hip dysplasia is genetically deter-
mined (inheritable), and that greater accuracy in detecting the
condition comes with maturity in the dog, it behooves the breeder
to take into account the radiographs obtained of the parents and
grandparents after they had reached two years, as well as the two-
year radiographs of the pair being considered for breeding.*

Procedure

The accepted technique for hip dysplasia examination[16,71] is to
position the dog "belly up." With the dog on its back and symmetrical (breastbone directly over spine, body straight, and an
imaginary line drawn from hip to hip being perpendicular to the
spine) a proper film can be made. Most dogs are not used to lying
in this position and having their limbs "stretched," so veterinarians
customarily prefer to tranquilize the dog in order to get a high
quality radiograph. Most agree that today's tranquilizers are so
safe and effective that there is little need to anesthetize a dog.[68]

When the radiography includes a wedge* view as well as a
standard view, tranquilizers may work satisfactorily to prevent discomfort and voluntary tension, but I have found anesthesia to be
necessary in the majority of cases due to the reaction of even a
drugged dog when the extra and considerable force is applied.

It is a fairly common practice to manipulate and palpate (feel)
the hip joints for any sign of laxity (looseness) or luxation (more
complete separation of the femur from the acetabulum) prepara-
tory to or following radiography. It is generally accepted in the
profession that "Radiologic examination alone is often inadequate
for hip dysplasia diagnosis, prognosis, and for selection of breeding stock. Palpation in conjunction with radiographic examination
can be helpful."[75]

Other Suggestions

The dog owner is advised to clarify ahead of time what size,
number, and quality of radiographs he wants. Usually your veterinarian will want to keep a copy for his own records. If one is to be

---

*Also known as the "fulcrum X-ray": a technique in radiographing wherein the
hips are subjected to a force by wedging a fulcrum between the legs near the
torso, then taking the picture while the stifles are pressed toward each other and
the femoral heads thus levered out of the sockets if they are loose.

sent to the OFA or to a prospective buyer, a second sheet of film can be put into the cassette. If you want an additional copy for your own files, he should know about it at the beginning.

It is a good practice not to feed the dog for at least six hours prior to your appointment, twice as long if anesthesia is to be used, and even then only a light meal. Water should be withheld for six hours in any case. Food may be vomited when the dog is tranquilized, and is a greater problem if it happens during anesthesia. Safety is not so much the concern as just making a big mess.

The size of the radiograph should be acceptable to OFA: for most breeds, the 14 x 17-inch film is desired so the pelvis, femurs, and stifles will appear on the film. The dog is positioned so that the center of the X-ray beam passes through the center of the pelvis. The legs are made parallel, the stifles rotated so the patellae (knee-caps) are directly over the depressions made between the condyles (knobs) at the stifles (knees). While applying a twisting motion, one exerts considerable tension on the legs while another pulls the thorax, forelegs, and head in the opposite direction. This keeps the dog from rolling to one side, insures symmetry, and makes it easier to put the femurs in a parallel, horizontal position. Sometimes a veterinarian will use ropes and tape to keep the dog in the right position and immobile while he and his assistant step behind lead-lined doors and flip the switch. The AVMA Panel on Hip Dysplasia has suggested some specific directions for positioning dogs.[71]

Identification of the film should be made with radiopaque markers and should give the dog's name and identification such as tattoo and/or AKC number, the owner's name, and the name of the radiologist or veterinarian. In addition, and a step most often forgotten, the right or left side of the dog should be identified. The fact that the dog is tattooed should be noted somewhere on the radiograph. The OFA supplies an application card to be included when mailing the radiograph.

Tattooing

While the dog is tranquilized, it can easily be tattooed for more positive control and identification. I have made it a practice of tattooing the AKC number on the dog's belly where the least hair is so as not to obscure it. Others, especially those registering their dogs with the National Dog Registry (NDR), use a social security number. This is sufficient for a dog that is not likely to be sold, and whose owner wishes to rely on the NDR being well enough known through their advertising and exposure to veterinarians that the lost dog would be reported and traced back to its home.

Wedge Technique

Subluxation and joint laxity have been used interchangeably in the literature, and in most instances mean the same thing. However, it could be said that subluxation is a visual record of laxity. The word luxation is used to describe a rather complete separation of the acetabulum and the femoral head. Joint laxity, especially in young dogs, may not always appear on the radiograph, hence the wedge or fulcrum method[3,33] is used to discover if the hip joints are loose.

Fig. 2-1. The author (left) and Dr. Charles Young prepare to make a pelvic radiograph using a compressed roll of cotton as a wedge or fulcrum. Legs are rotated and forced together at the hocks to lever femoral heads out of hip sockets if looseness is present.

photo by J. Lanting

A standard, unopened, compressed roll of cotton or a can of similar size is often used as the wedge, about 10 cm. (four inches) in diameter for a large dog. The roll used as the fulcrum is placed between the dog's legs on one of its flat sides (upright) and as close to the torso as possible (the medical term is "proximal"), pushing the scrotum forward and up in the case of a male patient. This allows the person rotating and pulling the legs to use the fulcrum to adduct the legs (force them toward each other) at the hocks and stifles and thus apply an abducting (separating) force at the ends in the sockets. It has been my experience that more effort is required to rotate so that the patellae remain over the midline of the stifles than is necessary without the wedge.

While a wedge-normal set of hips will not move measurably, joints with some degree of laxity will show subluxation with this technique: the femoral heads will move just so far out, then the tendonous tissue surrounding and making up part of the joint will prevent further dislocation. One hip may show a greater degree of subluxation than its opposite, though usually the condition is fairly symmetrical. [88]

In the older dog, wedge radiography has no practical advantage over standard-view radiography. As seen in Table I, when dogs reach two to three years of age, there is not much of a percentage of the population left that will develop dysplasia which have not already been diagnosed on a standard film. The value to the breeder in using wedge radiographs and comparing them to standard ones taken at the same session is that the younger dogs can be better screened for the disease. In other words, more information useful in making sell/keep/cull decisions is available. Some proponents of the technique claim that reliable prediction of future hip status can be had as early as four months, which is not really an excessive length of time to hold onto promising pups before selling them to show- or breeding-homes. In any case, it is true that the more information one has, the better his guarantees will be.

Hip Registry in Other Countries

Diagnosis, registry, and control of hip dysplasia are being carried out in a number of countries. Canadians use either the OFA or an evaluation by the University of Guelph, Ontario. There is a pan-Scandinavia ad hoc committee which has submitted suggestions to Scandinavian kennel clubs concerning registration/identi-

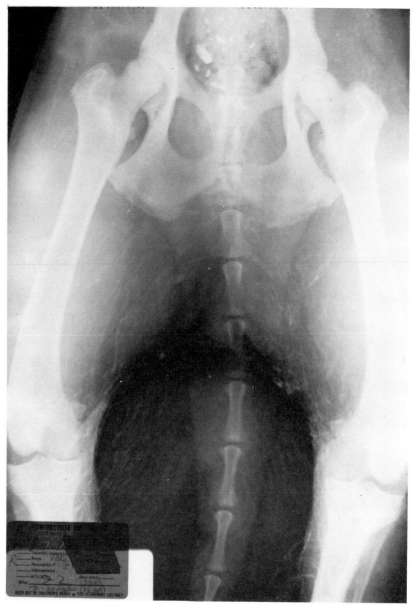

Fig. 2-2. Female from the author's normal "Z" litter,   wedge radiographed at 33 weeks. Note positions of cotton-roll wedge and patellas. In a young or small dog it is difficult to get femurs parallel, patellas centered, and the wedge placed close to the torso.

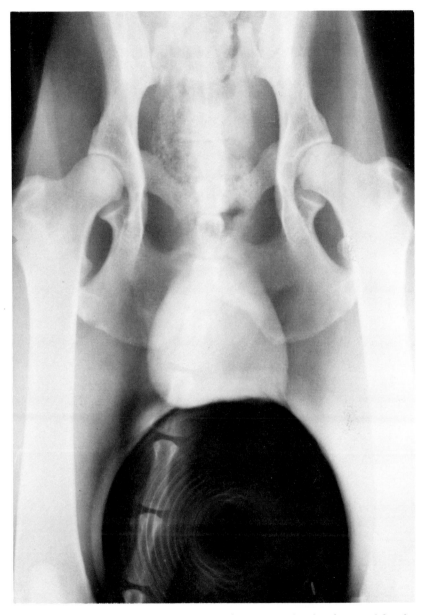

Fig. 2-3. Eko-Lan's Harry-O, OFA normal German Shepherd owned by the author. Wedge radiographed at two years of age. Standard view radiograph was taken at the same time and was identical in joint space. Note patellas are well positioned over center of stifle.

fication, radiography, and progeny testing, adding a very interesting mental or temperament test. In Western Australia, a grading system of A, B, C, D, E, and F is used to classify radiographs, in decreasing order of desirable hip joint configuration. Germany has a relatively long history of radiography, and control is largely a matter for the individual national breed clubs. The largest such club, the SV (Shaferhund Verein) is roughly equivalent to the German Shepherd Dog Club of America (GSDC of A) plus certain features of the AKC and the OFA for good measure.

In the SV, the reading of radiographs and the classification of hip status are in the hands of one man. Certification is referred to as "the 'a' stamp" because a dog of one year or older whose hip joints pass minimum requirements has a triangular stamp with an "a" in it affixed to its pedigree. Until recently, the "a" stamp was considered equivalent to an OFA number, but with OFA's adoption of a two-year minimum age and with improved communications between the SV, the GSDC of A, and the OFA, the SV has modified its rating system; there are now five categories, which will be discussed further in a later chapter.

Chapter 3
Prevalence

At the time the Eye Dog Foundation of California started a new program to reduce hip dysplasia, they were experiencing an incidence of 55 percent dysplastic dogs, most of these being German Shepherd Dogs, an ideal breed for guide work.[2,7] This percentage is probably a little more indicative of the actual incidence than OFA's statistics might lead one to imagine, since radiographs sent to the OFA are screened for the obviously dysplastic dogs by the veterinarian taking the picture and by the owner who might be reticent about paying for an OFA evaluation of a film on such a dog.[80] A greater proportion of radiographs are presumably sent to the SV than to the OFA, because the SV has the power to grant or deny breeding (registration) rights.

Whatever the actual percentage of dysplastic individuals among purebred dogs, it will probably decrease considerably in the coming years, thanks to the OFA and greater awareness on the part of breeders and buyers. A classification of pelvic radiographs in breeds with more than 100 evaluations was made by the OFA prior to 1972.[47] Because less than 70 percent of the dysplastic dogs could be identified at twelve months,[36] and because many of the more than one hundred breeds recognized by the AKC were not included in the study, I am not listing the recorded percentages of dysplastic dogs in that study. The basis for such percentages is inadequate for any degree of accuracy. But a tabulation of breeds in descending order of HD frequency will be of interest when we get into hip dysplasia's relation to body type and growth rate in the chapter on etiology (cause).

A five-year study[65] reported in 1972 tabulated the relative risk of hip dysplasia by breeds, with the following order of decreasing risk or incidence. The "R value" can be interpreted as the number of times more common HD is for that breed than for the general canine population.

TABLE II: FREQUENCY OF HD BY BREED (EARLY STATISTICS)

1. Saint Bernard	19. Irish Setter
2. Newfoundland	20. Keeshond
3. Bullmastiff	21. Great Dane
4. Old English Sheepdog	22. Samoyed
5. English Setter	23. Vizsla
6. English Springer Spaniel	24. Alaskan Malamute
7. Norwegian Elkhound	25. Great Pyrenees
8. Akita	26. Labrador Retriever
9. Chesapeake Bay Retriever	27. Doberman Pinscher
10. Golden Retriever	28. Puli
11. German Shepherd Dog	29. Wirehaired Pointing Griffon
12. Rottweiler	30. Standard Schnauzer
13. Gordon Setter	31. Dalmatian
14. Standard Poodle	32. Irish Wolfhound
15. Giant Schnauzer	33. German Shorthaired Pointer
16. Brittany Spaniel	34. Siberian Husky
17. Rhodesian Ridgeback	35. Belgian Tervuren
18. Weimeraner	36. Afghan Hound

While the percentage of dysplastic dogs in each breed in the above report were not accurate (apparently only the dogs showing clinical signs were radiographed), it is interesting to note that the average R-value for giant breeds (over 36.3 Kg) was about 10, that of large breeds about three or four, medium (9-18 Kg) breeds 0.2, and 0.2 again for small breeds. (Multiply by 2.2 to get weight in pounds.) The significance of this picture will be discussed later,

TABLE III.   RELATIVE RISK BY BREED

BREED	SIZE CATEGORY	R-VALUE
Saint Bernard	Giant	9.9
Chesapeake Bay Retriever	Large	5.8
Golden Retriever	Large	5.0
Labrador Retriever	Large	4.3
German Shepherd Dog	Large	4.2
Samoyed	Large	4.0
English Setter	Large	2.4
Toy & Miniature Poodle	Small	0.2
Cocker Spaniel	Medium	0.1

but for now it should be noted that hip displasia is more common in certain breeds which are similar in size, conformation, and other characteristics, and not as prevalent in breeds of quite different size and type.

The question: "How prevalent is hip dysplasia in my breed?" may never be answered with a constant figure. For one reason, methods of determining the percentage (age at radiographing, wedge vs. standard view, etc.) have been and will be revised. Secondly, popularity changes result in population variances and consequently in the number of radiographs submitted for evaluation; the larger the number, the more accurate the statistic. And most importantly, awareness on the parts of veterinarians, breeders, and the general public, coupled with selective breeding, will reduce the relative occurrence over a period of time. It is necessary that veterinarians especially, and dog writers as well, keep the pressure up in bringing the problem and solutions before the public.

By 1972 the OFA had found that, according to information in their files, Saint Bernards had 45 percent of their representatives dysplastic, with figures of 25 percent each for German Shepherd Dogs, Golden Retrievers, and Chesapeake Bay Retrievers, and 15 percent for Labrador Retrievers.[46] Because of the screening mentioned in the first paragraph of this chapter, twice the above numbers would be much closer to actuality in the general population.

Statistics compiled[2] in the early 1960's and into the latter part of that decade showed the incidence in German Shepherd Dogs to be about 80 percent, though this figure may be high because many dogs which did not show symptoms were not brought to the veterinarian for diagnosis. Less than 30 percent of the Afghan Hounds had hip dysplasia in those years, but with the tremendous increase in popularity of that showy breed, the figure has risen to close to 50 percent. The same thing happened with the Doberman Pinscher[44] which, back in the 40's and 50's was unpopular, characterized as a mean, vicious dog. But it had good hips, because it was bred and selected for specific working abilities, including agility, endurance, and jumping power. Breeders got rid of the "bad" disposition, and the incidence of hip dysplasia doubled in some 20 years.

In a one-year study[23] of "a"-stamp radiographs made and evaluated in Germany of 5,475 German Shepherd Dogs from

November 1, 1974 to October 31, 1975, about 13 percent of the
males and for some strange reason* a significantly different figure
of 21.6 percent of the bitches were considered free of hip dysplasia. Over 33 percent of the males and about 36 percent of the
bitches were considered suspicious. Those "free" of HD (17.6 percent of both sexes combined) represent a population percentage
far different from the 66 percent "normal" statistic derived from
reading the radiographs of nearly 4,000 U.S. German Shepherd
Dogs of approximately one year of age.[46] When one weighs a
probable lenience built into a radiograph evaluation of a year-old
dog against a stricter standard in the recent German classification,
the early OFA figure of 66 percent normals in German Shepherd
Dogs is too high, and the German 17.6 percent figure (more
recent) is too low. Some of those rated "suspicious" would possibly fall into the normal category at two years or more, but most
would likely not.

---

*Perhaps because of their age (as young as one year) and males growing faster,
some of the "a" females classified as free of dysplasia may have shown hip dysplasia if radiographed at a later age. One year of age just doesn't give enough
accuracy.

There is considerable variation in radiologic appearance of normal and dysplastic hips in various breeds of dogs. There is a risk that any deviation from the appearance of what is a normal hip joint for a German Shepherd Dog, for example, may be erroneously interpreted as HD or the same degree of dysplasia; differences between breeds should be taken into consideration. The OFA has used such phrases as "normal for age and breed."

A study reported by R. Scartazzini in 1972 involved a number of breeds, with many examples of each. Radiographs were made in both the usual ventro-dorsal position and the so-called Frog-leg position (with legs flexed).

Saint Bernards had curved cranial borders on the acetabula, normal shape and depth to both acetabula and femoral heads, but obvious subluxation (joint laxity). In this breed abnormal shape of hip joints may have greater importance, at least relative to that in other breeds, than the looseness of the head in the socket. In almost all other breeds, there was a better correlation between shape and subluxation.

In the German Shepherd, the acetabulum's cranial border is slightly curved, with the lateral part pointing cranially, instead of in the caudal direction as in the Saint. In the Rottweiler, Labrador, and Boxer, the border curves and slants in varying degrees, and in the Bernese Mountain Dog it is straight.

Tightness varies a great deal between typical specimens of each breed: the phenomenon of good form with loose joints under anaesthesia was not seen in the other breeds in the study.

Saints and Bernese Mountain Dogs had the deepest sockets, Labs and Boxers the most shallow, with Shepherds and Rottweilers in between.

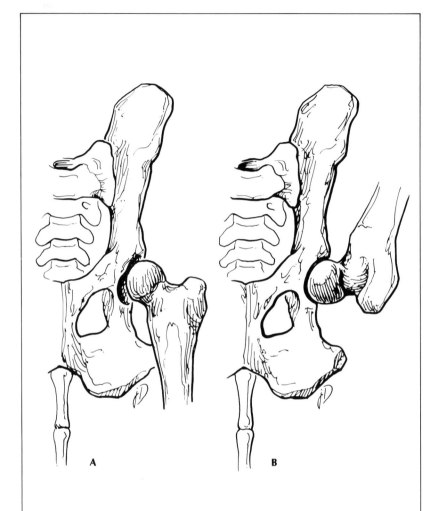

Fig. 3-1. Representative view of a one-year old Saint Bernard. Pelvis is relatively wide, acetabulum is deep and well-developed, and acetabular rim straight.
A. Standard view with legs extended. Considerable joint laxity obvious.
B. Same dog viewed with legs flexed. In both views the femoral head looks good, but in this position it appears to be perfectly seated in the acetabulum.

Chapter 4
Severity:
Grading the Radiograph

The SV System

In Germany, the SV now recognizes five categories in regard to hip dysplasia as seen on the radiograph, the first three of which can lead to the "a" stamp on the dog's pedigree: [19]

1. free of hip dysplasia (changed in 1975 to "normal");
2. suspicious of hip dysplasia (changed in 1975 to "almost normal");
3. slight hip dysplasia (changed in 1975 to "still permissible");
4. moderate hip dysplasia;
5. severe hip dysplasia.

Dr. Joseph Giardina was invited to review in 1974 the current SV radiographs along with Dr. Brass' evaluations, and was of the opinion [23] that the SV's category 1 would be equivalent to the OFA's "normal-excellent" rating, while many in SV category 2 might fall into category 3 if radiographed at age two or older. Of course, many might be given a good or fair normal rating by OFA also. The OFA would not likely certify "a"-stamp dogs of category 3. The SV prohibits dogs of categories 4 and 5 from being bred, something which is impossible in the U.S. because of the structure and authority limits of the AKC.

The OFA System

Following is the present (1980) descriptive grading or classification system employed by the OFA:

Excellent hip joint conformation—superior hip joint conformation as compared with other individuals of the same breed and age.

Good hip joint conformation—well-formed hip joint conformation as compared with other individuals of the same breed and age.

Fair hip joint conformation—minor irregularities of hip joint conformation as compared with other individuals of the same breed and age.

Borderline hip joint conformation—marginal hip joint conformation of indeterminate status with respect to hip dysplasia at this time.

Mild hip dysplasia—radiographic evidence of minor dysplastic change of the hip joints.

Moderate hip dysplasia—well-defined radiographic evidence of dysplastic changes of the hip joints.

Severe hip dysplasia—radiographic evidence of marked dysplastic changes of the hip joints.

The first three OFA classifications make a dog eligible for a breed OFA certification number if it is 24 months or older at the time of radiography. In addition to reporting the classification, the OFA report may comment on other radiographic findings such as ununited anconeal process (if films of elbows are sent as well), condition of stifles and spine, and miscellaneous findings.

The Schnelle Grading System

In 1954 it was suggested[82] that the veterinary profession substitute the term "hip dysplasia" for "congenital dislocation of the hip" in order to conform to the terminology used for the disorder in homo sapiens. At the same time there was proposed a classification of the degrees of the disease as revealed by X-rays, and four grades were arbitrarily chosen to represent points along a spectrum from normal to severely luxated. It must be emphasized that such a system was and is designed for use by the veterinarian, especially the radiologist, not the breeder. The reason it is presented in this work is because it is still in common use and many veterinarians still use the numbers one through four when talking with their clients.

Although the proponent of this system gradually deviated from it in the later years of his life,[79] it became a valuable tool for veterinarians and breeders who wished to communicate without sending copies of radiographs each time they tried to describe a certain degree of hip dysplasia. The grading of one through four (plus normal) tells something about the amount of separation of femoral heads from the acetabulum, but nothing about the pain and severity of the disease otherwise. There are some who feel there may be a clue, however inconclusive, to the dog's genotype; i.e., the higher numbers may correspond to a greater number of genes contributing to hip dysplasia.[44] This is a matter of controversy; many veterinarians believe that the degree of the defect as seen on the radiograph tells very little about the genotype, or the genetic makeup of that dog. Briefly, then, and incompletely for the veterinarian but adequately for most owners, following are descriptions[14] and illustrations of the four grades of HD in the old system as compared with normal hips.

Normal joints are characterized by smooth, rounded femoral heads and no evidence of erosion in the acetabulum, plus a fit that can be described as "beautiful," especially after the viewer has seen many bad ones. When looking at the joints illustrated in this text, bear in mind that when it comes to describing abnormal joints, some veterinarians may put more emphasis on secondary bony changes than on joint space between head and acetabulum, and vice-versa.[55]

Grade 1 dysplastic hips usually show a small amount of laxity, although it is a lot easier to spot this in more severe cases. Laxity or joint space may not be well-correlated with secondary bone changes (remodelling, arthritis) in the young dog. Grade 1 hips frequently show some small bony outgrowths (exostoses) where the head and neck of the femur meet, as viewed from the caudal (tail) side, seldom on the cranial side. It might be a good idea to ask your veterinarian, if he uses the Schnelle gradations, to describe the status in terms of the latest OFA classifications as well.

Grade 2 hips have the bony ridge-like growths extending a bit further along the dorsal section of the head-neck line and some thickening of the femoral neck between the head and the greater trochanter (the larger "shoulder-like" protrusion) as well as a more obvious joint space.

Grade 3 hips will generally show noticeable lipping of the femoral heads, resembling the tops of the tent stakes used at outdoor dog shows. Accompanying this is increased thickening of the neck and additional bony growth on the femur, as well as progressive erosion of the acetabulum and rounding of the rim with bone production that was evident in Grades 1 and 2 becoming worse in Grades 3 and 4. Erosion occurs in both the cup portion of the acetabulum and the rim. Subluxation becomes obvious to even the novice at this point.

Grade 4 hips show considerable remodelling (bone erosion, then production in an abnormal amount, place, or angle) all around the acetabular rim, with changes so severe in the cup that the acetabulum is extremely shallow compared to Grades 1 and 2. Adding that to the much-flattened heads, this grade presents a picture of luxation . . . practically no sockets, or at least not much proximity of the badly changed head to what is left of the acetabulum. Needless to say, the risk of trauma and pain and loss of over-all utility is greater as one goes from Grade 1 to Grade 4, with compensation and varying pain thresholds among individuals being taken into account.

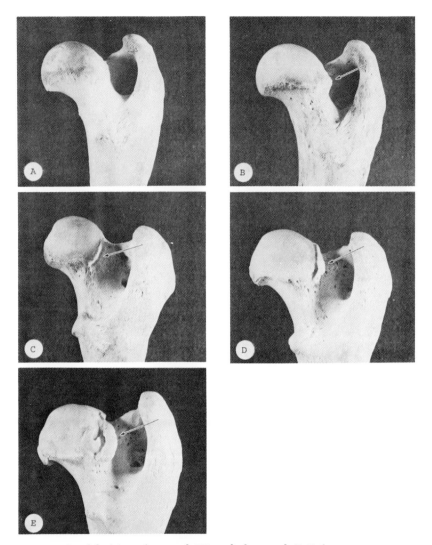

Fig. 4-1. Caudal views of normal (A) and abnormal (B-E) femurs, represent-ing progressive severity of pathologic changes used as a partial basis for assigning pathoanatomic scores of 0-4, respectively. Minimal changes (B) consisted of small exostoses of the femoral neck (arrow) on or just distal to the junction of the femoral head and neck. Larger exostoses (C-E) at that site (arrows) extended dorsally (C) and medially, resulting in lipping of the femoral heads (D and E). Specimens are right femurs.

Courtesy of G. H. Cardinet, III, D.V.M., Ph.D.
From Journ. Am. Vet. Med. Assn., Vol. 164., No. 6., p. 593. Mar. 15, 1974.

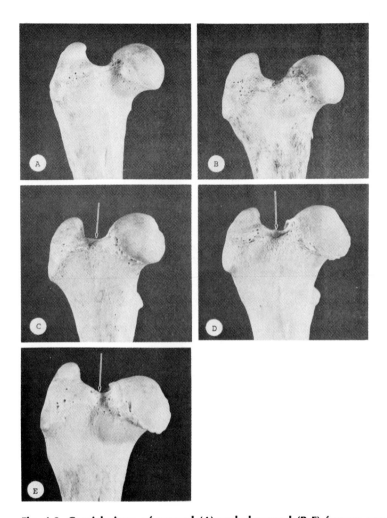

Fig. 4-2. Cranial views of normal (A) and abnormal (B-E) femurs, representing progressive severity of pathologic changes used as a partial basis for assigning pathoanatomic scores of 0-4, respectively. Femurs with minimal pathologic changes on the caudal aspect were essentially normal in appearance on the cranial aspect (B). Extension of exostoses from the caudal aspect dorsally were accompanied by bone production along the transverse line between the greater trochanter and femoral head (arrows.), which resulted in thickening of the femoral necks (C-E). Extension of exostoses cranially and medially resulted in lipping of the femoral heads (D and E). Specimens are right femurs.

From Cardinet, Journ. Am. Vet. Med. Assn.,
Vol. 164, No. 6., p. 594. Mar. 15, 1974.

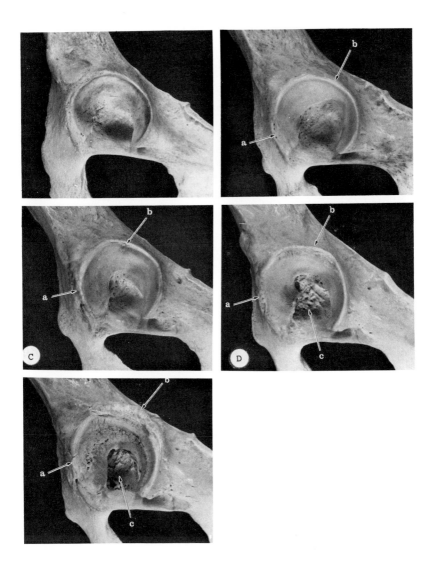

Fig. 4-3. Normal (A) and abnormal (B-E) acetabulums, representing the progressive severity of pathologic changes used as the basis for assigning pathoanatomic scores of 0-4, respectively. Erosion of (B) and erosion and bone production (C-E) were observed along the cranial (a) and dorsal (b) acetabular rims. As the changes become more severe, bone production, with filling of the acetabular fossa (c), was observed (D and E). Acetabulums with the most extensive changes also had erosion and bone production involving the remaining lunate surfaces (E). Specimens are left acetabulums.

Courtesy of G. H. Cardinett, III, D.V.M.,
from Journ. Am. Vet. Med. Assn., Vol. 164, No. 6, p. 595, Mar. 15, 1974.

Hip Dysplasia Commission of the FCI

Following are excerpts from a report of the Hip Dysplasia Commission of the Federation Cynologique Internationale (F.C.I.), a sort of federation of national all-breed clubs around the world.

In 1978, a series of radiographs with accompanying descriptions were agreed upon as representing normal hips (some member countries divide that category into excellent and good), a transitional or suspicious category, and three or four grades of obvious dysplasia.

Correct positioning for radiography, a standard identification form, anatomical nomenclature, minimum ages for various breeds to be certified. and other factors were standardized. Written and verbal communication between veterinarians and others regarding grades of dysplasia and just what constitutes "normal" will from now on be much more clearly understood.

The word "Anlage" is used for "Table," "Figure," or "Illustration."

Courtesy M. & H. Schaper Publishing Co.,
-Hanover, Germany.

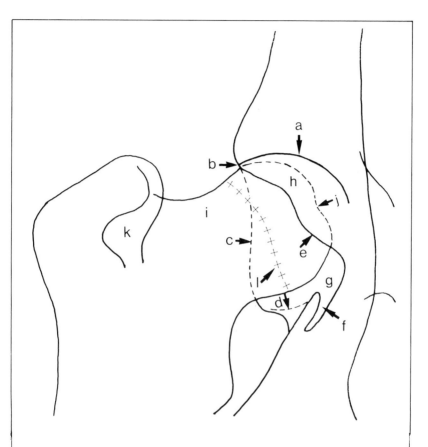

Abb. 1:

a. *margo acetabularis cranialis* – *cranial acetabular margin* – *kranialer Acetabulumrand*
b. *margo acetabularis craniolateralis* – *craniolateral rim* – *kraniolateraler Acetabulumrand*
c. *margo acetabularis dorsalis* – *lateral acetabular margin* – *dorsaler Acetabulumrand*
d. *margo acetabularis caudalis* – *caudal acetabular margin* – *kaudaler Acetabulumrand*
e. *margo acetabularis ventralis* – *ventral acetabular margin* – *ventraler Acetabulumrand*
f. *incisura acetabuli* – *acetabular notch*
g. *fossa acetabuli* – *acetabular fossa*
h. *caput femoris* – *femoral head* – *Femurkopf*
i. *collum femoris* – *femoral neck* – *Femurhals*
j. *fovea capitis* – *Bandgrube*
k. *fossa trochanterica* – *trochanteric fossa*
l. *borderline head/neck* – *Übergang Kopf/Hals (+ + + + +)*

Beschreibung der HD-Grade für Hunde im Alter von 1 bis 2 Jahren unter der Voraussetzung einer korrekten Lagerung in Position I.*)

Description of classes, appicable to dogs, aged between one and two years, provided correct positioning in Position I.*)

Kein Hinweis für Hüftgelenkdysplasie

Der Femurkopf und das Acetabulum sind kongruent und der Winkel nach Norberg (in Pos. I) ist 105 oder größer. Der kraniolaterale Rand des Acetabulum zeigt sich scharf oder in geringem Maße abgerundet. Der Gelenkspalt ist eng und gleichmäßig. Bei **hervorragenden** Hüftgelenken umgreift der kraniolaterale Azetabulumrand den Femurkopf etwas weiter nach laterokaudal.

No signs of hip dysplasia

The femoral head and the acetabulum are congruent and the acetabular angle according to Norberg (adapted for Pos. I) is 105 or more. The craniolateral rim appears sharp or slightly rounded. The jointspace is narrow and even. In **excellent** hipjoints the craniolateral rim encircles the femoral head somewhat more in laterocaudal direction.

Übergangsform (verdächtig für HD)

Entweder sind Femurkopf und Acetabulum in geringem Maße inkongruent mit einem Norbergwinkel (in Pos. I) von 105 oder größer.
oder der Norbergwinkel ist kleiner als 105, wobei der Femurkopf und das Acetabulum kongruent sind. Geringe Unschärfen am kranialen, kaudalen oder dorsalen Azetabulumrand können vorhanden sein.

Transitional or borderline hipjoints

The femoral head and the acetabulum are slightly incongruent and the acetabular angle according to Norberg (adapted for Pos. I) is 105 or more, **or** the acetabular angle according to Norberg is less than 105 and the femoral head and the acetabulum are congruent. Minor irregularities in margo acetabularis cranialis, caudalis or dorsalis may be present.

Leichte HD

Femurkopf und Acetabulum sind inkongruent, der Norbergwinkel ist größer als 100 und/oder der kraniolaterale Rand des Acetabulum ist in geringem Maße abgeflacht. Unschärfen oder höchstens geringe Anzeichen osteoarthrotischer Veränderungen des kranialen, kaudalen oder dorsalen Azetabulumrandes können vorhanden sein.

Mild hip dysplasia

The femoral head and the acetabulum are incongruent, the acetabular angle according to Norberg is more than 100 and/or there is a slightly flattened craniolateral rim. Irregularities or no more than slight signs of osteoarthrotic changes of the margo acetabularis cranialis, caudalis or dorsalis may be present.

Mittlere HD

Deutliche Inkongruenz zwischen Femurkopf und Acetabulum mit Subluxation. Norbergwinkel größer als 90 (nur als Referenz).
Abflachung des kraniolateralen Azetabulumrandes und/oder osteoarthrotische Merkmale.

Moderate hip dysplasia

Obvious incongruency between the femoral head and the acetabulum with subluxation. Acetabular angle according to Norberg more than 90 (only as reference). Flattening of the craniolateral rim and/or osteoarthrotic signs.

Schwere HD

Auffällige dysplastische Veränderungen an den Hüftgelenken, wie z.B. Luxation oder deutliche Subluxation, Norbergwinkel unter 90, deutliche Abflachung des kranialen Azetabulumrandes, Deformierung des Femurkopfes (pilzförmig, abgeflacht) oder andere osteoarthrotische Merkmale.

Severe hip dysplasia

Marked dysplastic changes of the hipjoints, such als luxation or distinct subluxation, acetabular angle according to Norberg less than 90, obvious flattening of the margo acetabularis cranialis, deformation of the femoral head (mushroomshape, flattening) or other signs of osteoarthrosis.

Diese Klassifizierung beruht ausschließlich auf den röntgenologisch erfaßbaren Erscheinungen. Sie ist so eindeutig wie möglich formuliert und sollte für die Beurteilung aller Rassen dienen.

This classification has been made up on account of the radiological features only. It is as objective as it possibly could be and should be applied to all breeds.

---

*) Dieses Klassifizierungsschema kann auch für die Beurteilung älterer Hunde Anwendung finden. Sekundäre arthrotische Veränderungen sollten dabei unter Berücksichtigung des Alters bewertet werden.

*) This classification scheme may be adopted for older dogs, but secondary arthrotic changes have then to be evaluated according to the age of the dog.

Liste der HD-Beurteilungsstellen in den der F.C.I. angeschlossenen Ländern
List of HD-panels in the F.C.I.-countries

BELGIEN:
Kommissie voor heupdysplasie bij de hond
Dr. E. Timmermans
Belgische Syndicale Dierenartsen Vereiniging
Herzieningslaan 24
1070 Brussel

DÄNEMARK:
Dr. Bent Riis
Poppelstykket 11
DK-2450 Copenhaqen S.

DEUTSCHLAND:
1. Prof. Dr. W. Brass
   Klinik für kleine Haustiere
   Bischofsholer Damm 15
   3000 Hannover

2. Prof. Dr. K. Löffler
   Universität Hohenheim
   Holdingerstraße 3
   7441 Wolfschlugen

3. Prof. Dr. H. Müller, Dr. Reinhard
   Chirurgische Veterinärklinik der Justus-Liebig-Universität
   Frankfurter Straße 94
   6300 Gießen

4. Prof. Dr. L. Felix Muller, Prof. Dr. Chr. Saar
   Klinik für kleine Haustiere
   Bitterstraße 8–12
   1000 Berlin 33

5. Dr. Christine Niessen
   Tierärztliches Institut der Universität
   Groner Landstraße 2
   3400 Göttingen

6. Prof. Dr. H. Schebitz
   Chirurgische Universitätstierklinik
   Veterinärstraße 13
   8000 München 22

7. Dr. Hermann Wurster
   Fachtierarzt für Chirurgie
   Pfeseerstraße 15
   8900 Augsburg

DOMINIKANISCHE REPUBLIK:
Dra. Mireya Scheker
Apartado Postal 402
Santo Domingo

FINNLAND:
Prof. Dr. S. Paatsama
Risto Rytintie 17
00570 Helsinki 57

FRANKREICH:
Commission Zootechnique de la Société Centrale Canine
Prof. J. Coulon
École Vétérinaire 2
Quai Chaveau 63337
Lyon Cedex 1

JUGOSLAWIEN:
Prof. Dr. M. Tadić
Faculté de Méd. Vét.
Boulevard JNA 18
11000 Beograd

LUXEMBURG:
Dr. J. Georg
15. rue Emile Mayrisch
Esch sur Alzette

NIEDERLANDE:
Kommissie voor Heupdysplasie-onderzoek bij de hond
N. A. van der Velden
Yalelaan 17
Utrecht

NORWEGEN:
Norsk Diagnosesentral for hofteleddsdysplasi
Dr. Petter Heim
Bjerkealleen 10
Hovik

SCHWEDEN:
Dr. Lars Andell
Gudby gard. S-19400.
Upplands Vasby

SCHWEIZ:
1. Prof. Dr. U. Freudiger
   Med. Tierklinik
   Langgass Straße 124
   3001 Bern

2. Kant. Tierspital Zurich
   Prof. Dr. A. Müller
   Winterthurerstraße 260
   8057 Zürich

From *Kleintier Praxis.* 23, 169-180 (1978),
Verlag M. & H. Schaper Hannover.

The OFA vs. the SV System of Evaluating a Hip Radiograph

At one time the OFA made their determination of the hip status when the animal reached 12 months of age. Later, research brought forth the fact that at 12 months of age the reliability factor was only in the 70 percentile range, which meant that about 30 percent of those animals who received an OFA certification at 12 months of age would develop H.D. at a later date. Consequently, the OFA raised the age to 24 months in making its determination for certification. At 24 months the reliability factor is in the 90 percentile range.

In Germany, the "a" stamp is issued based on the reading of a radiograph taken when the animal has reached 12 months of age. Also, the "a" stamp is issued in three categories, normal, suspicious, and light hip dysplasia. (The last category is like saying that a woman is a little pregnant!)

Therefore, the "a" stamp should never be judged equivalent to an OFA certification because of the age differences, and also because of the differences in the categories. People who obtain an "a" stamped dog should have this animal radiographed again at 24 months of age and determine whether the animal is indeed normal.

Dr. Joseph F. Giardina,
Veterinary practitioner,
Chairman of Veterinary Liaison
and Hip Dysplasia Committee,
German Shepherd Dog Club of America

Chapter 5
Practical
Aspects

The Service Dog

The U.S. Air Force, through a procurement department, trains most of the dogs for our Armed Services, and nearly all dogs used by the U.S. government are sent to Lackland AFB near San Antonio, Texas, where they learn the arts of sniffing out explosives and drugs, guarding property, sentry duty, and anti-personnel work. Much of the work is rigorous, requiring excellent to fair hip joint configuration, depending on the individual dog's specialty. To wait until a dog is two years old and OFA-certifiable would mean missing a year of service as well as decreased likelihood of availability, so "defense dogs" are purchased or accepted as donations as early as one year of age. While some up to three years old are also accepted, the amount of time and money invested in training mandates selection as early as possible. Prospects for military service are radiographed upon or before arrival at Lackland, and normal or near-normal hips are accepted; the dog then undergoes other tests to determine if it can be taught to bite and hold, if it takes to scent work, and other qualifying tests.

The Guide Dog

Schools that train guide dogs for the blind are much concerned about hip status as well as characteristics suitable for the peculiar type of work demanded of their students. There is much variance from one school to another: some get all or most of their dogs via donations, others prefer to breed their own stock and place them in 4H homes or similar environments until about the age of one year, at which time they are radiographed and begin training if they have the hips and aptitude desired. It is interesting to note that the breeds which are most used for guide work are among those at the tops of the lists for prevalence of hip dysplasia, excluding the giant breeds which would not be suitable because of their height and the resulting height of the harness. German Shepherd Dogs, Golden Retrievers, and Labrador Retrievers are some of the "leaders" in both senses of the word.

The fact that dogs are pressed into service, to borrow a wartime term, at the tender age of one year, before all of the dysplastic ones can be identified by standard methods, necessitates better selection techniques in order to cut financial and temporal losses. More work along such lines as wedge radiography, progeny testing, etiology, genetics, and prediagnostic techniques is needed; this means money. Foundations such as the John Olin Foundation have contributed generously, government agencies such as the National Institute of Health have helped, and individuals have given much of their time and resources. If the reader desires to help, three excellent organizations are accepting donations which can be earmarked for research on hip dysplasia: The Morris Animal Foundation, the New York State Veterinary College, and the Orthopedic Foundation for Animals.*

---

*Morris Animal Foundation, 531 Guaranty Bank Bldg., Denver, CO 80202. N.Y. State Veterinary College, Cornell University, Ithica, N.Y. 14850. OFA. University of Missouri, Columbia, MO 65211.

Fig. 5-1. It is heartbreaking when a guide dog develops debilitating dysplasia after months of intense training or years of faithful service.

Photo courtesy of The Seeing Eye, Inc.,
Morristown, New Jersey

Contracts and Guarantees

The possibility of crippling hip dysplasia in later months of a puppy's life has been a bugaboo to breeders for some time. The buyer of a three-month old pup today typically wants some kind of assurance that he is getting value for his dollar, and has become accustomed to hearing about guarantees, and even consumer protection legislation.[44] Many national breed clubs have suggested bills of sale or contracts for their members to use, which usually guarantee the purchase against AKC-disqualifying faults (except in some pet contracts), poor health (with a couple of days or more in which to have the dog checked at a veterinarian's office), non-registrability, etc. *and* against "crippling hip dysplasia to one year of age." The contracts vary in number almost as do the breeders, but this last minimum statement on hips is finding its way into more and more agreements of purchase.

The Pet

Even the pet buyer may want a guarantee against hip dysplasia, and it should be made clear what the guarantee covers: clinical signs such as limping because of pain in the coxofemoral joint, or radiographic signs? Either way, there can be disagreement, but a written contract is better than none. Most dogs sold as pets and companions will not encounter heavy demands on their strength and stamina, and will live satisfactorily with a mild form of hip dysplasia. Remember, "there are wide variations in the individual (pain) response to the disease"[71] and I've seen many such as a Grade 2 dog which coped with a life of chasing horses in the snow while his Grade 1 littermate in a different home but the same neighborhood "complained" of some discomfort for a couple of months around one year of age. Generally, though, if a dysplastic dog, Grade 1 or 2, is given a warm place to sleep, and moderate exercise with a proper diet, it may do a great job as a companion with little if any problems due to its dysplasia.

The Dog in Competition

The dog sold to an obedience trial devotee should have at least borderline hips, though I've seen many, many with mild hip dysplasia in competition, and a few with a moderate level of the disease. But the strain of hours of practice, especially the jumping

Fig. 5-2. Strong, powerful hips are a requirement for dogs trained in advanced obedience or schutzhund.

Courtesy of Sue Barwig, Denver, Co.

encountered in the advanced classes, is easier on the dog with the better hips. Since most of the shock of landing after clearing the broad jumps or the hurdles is taken up by the front assembly, good elbows and shoulders may be more important than the utmost soundness in hips. When the jumping dog leaves the ground, it does so straight ahead, with both rear feet generally leaving the ground at the same time and no twisting effect. Also, much more thrust in jumping is provided by the front legs than most people would imagine.

Any estimate of a hypothetical dog's utility, of course, is a very unscientific generalization, but it must be said here that, depending upon the individual dog, the dysplastic canine may be a perfectly satisfactory companion and a useful partner. Steps the breeder can take to prevent hip dysplasia will be treated in Section IV.

HIP DYSPLASIA IN THE WORKING STOCK DOG

In 1976, the American Animal Hospital Association published a study by Doctors John Pharr and Joe Morgan, describing the occurrence of hip dysplasia in a breed known for its ability in herding livestock. In pre-machine eras, this work was said to require a great deal of stamina and excellence of health and utility. However, it seems that not all such working dogs were pressed to near their limits as has been popularly believed.

Dogs of the Australian Shepherd breed were selected for normal gait and for having had a pelvic radiograph made at one year or older. Additionally, they or their parents or grandparents were generally "employed" as stock dogs, with varying demands on them. Most were family pets as well and it is not likely any in this study had been overworked.

Of 23 dogs examined, 13 were radiographically normal at ages between 12 and 28 months (except for one first X-rayed at 76 months). Two of these under 1½ years old showed dysplasia upon second evaluations at 2 and 5 years age respectively. Two others rated "questionable" at 12 and 15 months, were dysplastic by 4 and 2½ years, respectively. There was even some joint laxity in two more dogs that were radiographically normal at 3 and 2 years of age. (See Chapter 2, "At What Age to Radiograph.")

Info from "Hip Dysplasia in Australian Shepherd Dogs."
by John W. Pharr, DVM and Joe Morgan, DVM.
Journ. Am. Animal Hosp. Assn., Vol. 12,
No. 4, July-Aug. 1976.

Photo courtesy of
Dr. John W. Pharr

Chapter 6
Theories
on the Cause(s)
of Canine Hip Dysplasia

Background

What causes hip dysplasia in dogs? Perhaps the question should be phrased in the plural: what are the causes of canine hip dysplasia? To answer that question, we must embark on a research journey analogous to the many searches for the headwaters of the Nile: we start at a point we know and work toward the unknown, from Alexandria past Cairo, to Khartoum and beyond, perhaps battling gnats and crocodiles all the way. One simply doesn't parachute to the answer; it can only be found by sweat and blood and tears. We can't completely answer the question today, but thanks to some excellent work done so far, we have several theories worth investigating and may someday be able to point to the source or sources of the river we presently navigate.

Working backwards from several points on the delta, investigators [1,8,12,21,25,67,85] have been pursuing the etiology* of hip dysplasia for many years. Theories have been proposed because certain facts were observed or deductions made, and frequently later data have seemed to deny the tentative conclusions reached.

Besides subluxation or joint laxity, early studies noted bone and joint changes characterized in the disorder. Hip dysplasia has been called "a condition in which subluxation of the femoral head leads to abnormal wear with erosion of the joint cartilage, thickening of the joint capsule, and formation of periarticular osteophytes** in early adulthood. The shape of the hip joint undergoes changes, the acetabulum becomes more shallow than normal, and the femoral head flattened." [60]

Many observers in the 1920's, 30's, and 40's proposed a congenital skeletal defect. Others put more emphasis on laxity or

---

*The study of causes, especially in regard to disease.
**Bony growths around the articulating or opposing joint surfaces.

instability at birth and during growth, interfering with normal development. A more recent study indicates *two* types of HD in man, one a multigenic* acetabular dysplasia, and the other caused by joint laxity. Still others have called hip dysplasia a collection of several or many diseases appearing as one.

Hormone Theories

In the late 50's and early 60's it was hypothesized that human infants with hip dysplasia had an abnormal pattern of excreting estrogens (female sex hormones) and a new clue was proffered to the world of medicine. However, attempts to duplicate and substantiate it in 1968 resulted in an inability to confirm such a pattern. A great deal of time and money was expended [10, 20, 27, 42] and the general conclusion is that hormones play a minor part, if any. Today it cannot be said that such biochemicals are involved in the cause of hip dysplasia in man or canine. [70]

Other Observations

While the above work on hormones was going on, some were emphasizing the roles of growth rate, adult size, and ratio of muscle to bone in the pelvis. [71,73,74] Invaluable information and direction were provided for later work and thought on the control of the disease in individual dogs, especially during their critical growth period before ossification (bone formation) is completed. A later chapter on feeding will cover this in more detail. Most veterinarians today feel that biomechanical balance, size, growth characteristics, and tissue strength are the only positive, inherited factors that can be listed as causes of hip dysplasia in the dog.

Congential Pectineus Myopathy* Theory

A number of veterinarians have studied changes in the pectineus muscle, one of the prominent muscles attached to the femur and pelvis. It can readily be seen in many dogs when the animal is lying on its back with its rear legs apart in a "frogleg" position (stifles abducted). [5, 15]

One theory advanced in 1969 [15] was that shortly after birth, the pectineus is composed of about 3 percent Type I muscle fibers

---

*Caused by or involving several genes.

and 97 percent Type II fibers, the two being differentiated by a specific cell staining technique. As the dog approaches sexual maturity, more fibers change so that the ratio is nearly 50/50. This theory held that in the pectineus, only Type II fibers are affected by a stunting or atrophy known as muscle fiber hypotrophy. The Type II fibers may fail to grow at a normal rate and most of them are considerably smaller than the other fibers in the muscle. This research has not been widely held to be valid, as it has not been satisfactorily duplicated by other workers. In opposition, Dr. Riser has said, "No such disease has ever been found in this muscle,"[68] noting that no myopathies* were present in either normal or dysplastic *adults* in the report.[70]

The myopathy theory was extended[2] to say that the inhibited growth of the pectineus at a time when the femur is continuing to lengthen (and quite rapidly) is analogous to a rubber band: the longer it is stretched out, the more resistance to further stretching it has. Because of the design of the muscle and the hip socket, the femoral head is thus levered or twisted out of the acetabulum, or at least more pressure is exerted on one portion of the acetabular rim than normally. As this progresses, the weight of the dog is more and more supported by the ligaments and tissues of the joint capsule instead of the cup of the acetabulum. These forces on the rim of the acetabulum[6] result in a degeneration of the structure into a dysplastic form.

Research in pectineus myopathy has been discontinued since 1972, at least in regard to reporting it in the literature, and the previous suppositions have not been substantiated to the satisfaction of most in the profession. Those who felt the theory warranted further investigation have asked: what causes the apparent myopathy? No such lesions were found in the other adductor muscles served by the same major nerve, the obturator nerve.[15] Workers could not establish a causal relationship between the pectineus muscles and hip dysplasia in one experiment[52] using the pelvic muscles from Labrador Retrievers, German Shepherd Dogs, Alaskan Malamutes, and Beagles. The relationship between hip dysplasia and any abnormality of the pectineus remains undefined.

---

*Myo-: muscle;   -pathy: pathological disease.

Forces on the Hip

Whether or not one agrees with the theory of pectineus muscle spasm as one of the internal factors tending to shift the angle of vector forces to less than 90° and thus change where much of the weight is supported, the fact is clear that joint laxity and a shallow acetabulum are the main characteristics of hip dysplasia. As a dysplastic pup grows, increased pressure is exerted on the joint capsule ligaments and on the rim of the acetabulum which has not yet fully ossified (become bone). Inflammation increases synovial fluid production, neutrophils, mucin, and insoluble collagen. Hemorrhage begins beneath periosteal surfaces and osteophytes form, with secondary degeneration known as arthritic changes.

In the normal hip, the acetabulum usually is deeper, covering more of the femoral head. The middle third of the rim retains its form, the ligaments are undamaged, and excessive looseness is absent. Ball and socket remain congruent.

If spasm is surgically prevented, or if pup is kept light in weight or prevented from putting weight on the hip, it still has no effect on the genetic pool. The individual will carry the same genes throughout life and can transmit those genes to its offspring.   *F. L. L.*

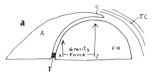

x———— y represents surface to bear weight of the normal hip
x⁻⁻ y represents surface to bear the same amount of weight

A—acetabulum   JC—Joint capsule (ligament)
C—Cartilage end of acetabular rim   T—Teres (round) ligament
FH—Femoral Head

Fig. 6-1. Forces on the hip socket.
a. Normal hip schematic. Good support, normal joint space between acetabulum and head, tight capsule, good form to acetabulum.
b. Dysplasia. Note increased joint space, stretched teres ligament and joint capsule, shallow acetabulum, and deformed cartilage. Surface (S) of femoral head will become flattened as weight is concentrated in that area.

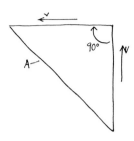

**Diagram of essential forces
on the hip joint.**

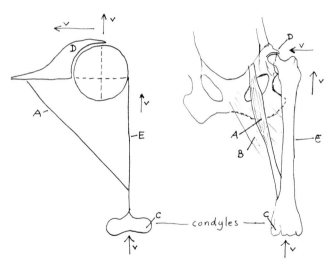

**Vector schematic of the
hip joint.**

**Sketch based on radiographs,
with vectors indicated.**

Fig. 6-2. Normal forces on the hip.
A—pectineus muscle
B—Adductor magnus muscle
C—Condyles at stifle

D—Acetabulum
E—Femur

From unpublished manuscript by J. W. Bardens, D.V.M.[5]
Reprinted with permission.

Spinal Lesion Theory

In spite of the pectineus muscle disease theory not being generally accepted, a number of veterinarians still believe HD to be at least partly a neuromuscular problem; i.e., the nervous system is somehow involved. Work conducted at the University of Georgia indicated spasm of the pectineus may be present, and electromyography further indicates the primary lesion to be located in the spinal cord. However, this has not been confirmed.[5]

Collagen Theory

It has been recently postulated that as increasing weight of the growing pup combines with joint laxity and a poor angle of insertion of the head into the acetabulum, inflammation of the capsule develops, with changes in the chemical nature of the joint fluids and in the collagen content. Collagen is the principal solid substance of white fibrous connective tissue, referred to as an intercellular cement that gives tissues their strength.[9] This theory, presently discounted by most of the veterinary profession, holds that with such inflammation, the ratio of soluble to insoluble "high quality" collagen decreases, hemorrhage occurs beneath the sheath of smooth tissue on the outer layer of bones, protuberances called osteophytes invade the area, and secondary arthritis begins. This theory, based in part on the ideas of Dr. Linus Pauling, holds that ascorbate (Vitamin C) is required for the production of collagen.

What basis is there for believing an insufficiency of ascorbate exists in dysplastic dogs? It has been claimed[83] that hypoascorbemia or scurvy is a genetic disease, not simply a dietary disturbance, and that ascorbate is much more than a trace vitamin. Signs of frank (clinical, obvious) scurvy appear in animals incapable of making their own ascorbic acid, but under conditions of extreme stress, even those that *can* produce it apparently cannot make enough, and signs of scurvy appear. When a heavy sled load under conditions of extreme cold and long hours resulted in symptoms of scurvy (insufficiency of ascorbate) in sled dogs, those symptoms disappeared when fresh seal meat including the livers was fed to the dogs.[13,61]

According to proponents of the collagen theory, a condition known as chronic *sub*clinical scurvy exists; symptoms are not as classical or obvious as they are in an acute, clinical manifestation.

They feel it is a basis of other complaints including a lack of resistance to a wide variety of conditions including feline rhinotracheitis, dermatitis, several viral diseases, etc. Stresses which may be sufficient to give rise to subclinical problems may not be high enough to elicit the more easily diagnosed signs of more severe scurvy.[42]

The theory that subclinical Vitamin C (ascorbate) deficiency may be at the root of the hip dysplasia problem has been unsubstantiated. Recent work at Cornell indicates nothing in this approach is beneficial in preventing or alleviating hip dysplasia.[68]

Growth Rate, Body Type

Attempts to find the cause of hip dysplasia led to many genetic studies and breeding programs, which will be enlarged upon in coming chapters, but it's worth mentioning again here that among the conclusions of such work was the observation that early rapid growth and weight gain were correlated with hip dysplasia.[71,74] Breed type has a definite influence: assuming that Saint Bernards have an extremely high incidence of hip dysplasia, then if one were to breed "Saints," or a dog that looks like a Saint Bernard, one will have to live with hip dysplasia to some extent. "Like produces like" is one relevant maxim; another is the old one about "if it walks like a duck, talks like a duck, etc., chances are it has some duck in it." It's very hard to find HD-free individuals in a breed that is so plagued with the disease. If one's heart is set on such a breed, one must be extreme in his demands for the most demanding radiographs and ruthless in his culling for future breeding partners.

Pelvic Bone Structure

A factor brought to light at the OFA Symposium in 1972[60] is the relative width of the pelvis and the related tilt of the acetabula. It was found that dogs with asymmetric pelves frequently developed unilateral hip dysplasia. Many with fractured femurs and resultant changes in the angle at which the head was supported by the roof of the socket had signs of degenerative disease and subluxation or luxation preferentially on the side which had decreased support. In other fractures the opposite effect was noted, when dysplasia was prevented in one hip by the pelvis healing in such a manner as to provide a better roof than had nature.

Measurements made on the stripped pelves of normal German Shepherd Dogs, dysplastic German Shepherd Dogs, Greyhounds, and Shepherd/Greyhound crosses, as well as on their radiographs and joint laxity, indicated that wider pelves were consistent with good hips and that the angle of the acetabula was generally more "horizontal" in the wider pelvis than in the narrow pelvis. This inward tilt of the sides of the pelvic cavity and palpatable joint instability apparently can exist independently as well as together and interdependently. Which means that there could be more than one cause of hip dysplasia! Generally, a slanting acetabular roof allows a lesser amount of joint laxity to initiate subluxation and to start the process of architectural changes in the femoral head and acetabular rim.

I like to use a butterfly as an illustration to describe the tilt of the pelvis just mentioned, since most people think only in terms of croup, which is a view from another angle. Imagine a butterfly perched on the croup of a dog, about midway between the two "hipbones" at the top and the two nearest the vent (anus). As the butterfly opens its wings, with the "viewer" standing at the dog's head, the wings make a very sharp V, an acute angle, at first; then as the wings continue to open, a right angle is formed, than an obtuse angle, until the wings are flat and opposed like the cylinders in an old Volkswagen going uphill. At some point in the motion, the wings roughly parallel the wide V of the pelvis of the dog the butterfly rests upon. If the wings (and pelvis) form an acute angle, one can visualize the femoral heads getting less support from the acetabula on the underside of the pelvic "wings." If the wings (and pelvis) approach a 180-degree angle, much more support can be imagined.

Years ago it was a commonly repeated supposition that the extreme angulation (a 90-degree angle between femur and lower leg bones) desired by many German Shepherd Dog judges and breeders was causing a great deal of the hip dysplasia. However, there are as many straight-stifle German Shepherd Dogs with HD as there are well-angulated ones with the disease, and just look at the incidence in the Saint Bernard, which is not usually thought of as having great "bend of stifle." While it was fashionable to talk about a "slinky" rear end[44] as the culprit, these same people didn't ask themselves why hip dysplasia was so low in the "slinky" cat. A sloping topline and a steep croup were also widely blamed, the former mostly an illusion due to the fad of posing a level-backed dog overstretched in the show ring. I have not made an extensive study of croup angle in relation to hip dysplasia, but I doubt if there is much of a connection, if any. In preparation for publication of this book, among the many sets of radiographs we made was a comparison of a German Shepherd bitch's croup with that of a Whippet male. The Whippet is a group-placing champion in two countries, has a Field Champion title for his excellence in lure coursing, and ran very well in straight-away racing. In short, he was built properly, the way a racing hound of top quality should be. The Shepherd bitch was the most nearly perfect example of her breed I had ever known, not only in regard to her intelligence and tough-as-nails yet affectionate temperament, but with excellent hip radiographs at six years of age, true movement, and effortless suspended gait. I'm not boasting, as I admit I wasn't her breeder. Radiographs made from the side with the dogs in "show poses" (hocks or metatarsal bones vertical) showed no significant difference in croup angle between the two animals. Whether the bitch had one foot slightly under her as in the ring, or both hocks vertical, made no difference in the croup angle; it tilted the whole pelvis just a little to the side when in the former pose, like an airplane beginning a right turn while maintaining the same angle of climb. It should be noted that a different conclusion was reached when comparing radiographs of a young flat-crouped Greyhound with a young German Shepherd Dog which apparently had a steep croup. However, those photographs[60] show the Shepherd standing with femurs pointing considerably under the dog, not vertical. There are individual variations in any breed, whether croup angle or other structural differences.

Getting back to the butterfly and the pelvic angle rather than the croup angle, it can be seen that the wider open the "wings," the wider the dog's hindquarters, other things being equal. The major conclusion of the 1972 Greyhound/Shepherd study was that "hip dysplasia is a developmental disease of multifactorial etiology. The shape of the pelvis is one factor, joint laxity is another."[28,29,60] We have found this in our own breeding experience, as exemplified by our K-4 bitch that had excellent radiographs (OFA-normal). She had wider hips, and seemed proportionally wider along her whole body than the average dog of her breed. Generally, those "broader in the stern" have given us the best radiographs.

Pelvic Muscle Mass

A positive correlation was found[71,73] between the prevalence of hip dysplasia and the relative amount of muscle in the area of the pelvis; three breeds were chosen as representative of the two extremes and a broad middle-ground in the occurrence of hip dysplasia. Track Greyhounds are somewhat smaller and of slightly different appearance than the AKC Greyhounds one is likely to see at a conformation (point) show. They are bred only for speed, and those failing to attain both the desire and the ability to win are culled, so that track breeders mimic nature in selection of the

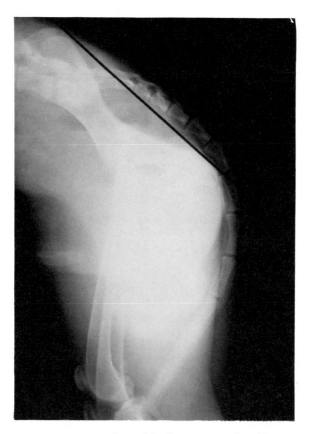

Fig. 6-3. Croup of an ideally structured Whippet. Contrary to popular notion, a result of an optical illusion caused by the racing dog's topline, the slope of a Whippet's croup is not steeper than that of a German Shepherd.

fittest. Hip dysplasia is not found in these dogs. Another non-AKC-recognized breed is the July Foxhound, which breed is or was composed almost entirely of dysplastic individuals. The third breed in the study was the German Shepherd Dog, representative of nearly all other breeds in its excellent specimens, its grossly dysplastic specimens, and all shades in between. Additionally, it is the most popular breed world-wide. Neither July Foxhounds nor German Shepherd Dogs have been selected with much regard for musculature, hindquarters, or speed, although the picture is improving in the latter breed with the growth of Schutzhund training interest in the United States.

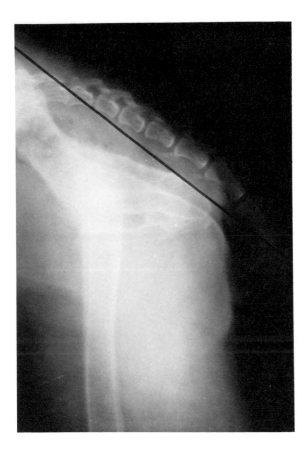

Fig. 6-4. German Shepherd bitch, posed with hocks and femurs vertical. Croup angle nearly identical to that of the Whippet.

Ninety-five dogs were radiographed, divided into six groups by breed and degree of hip dysplasia, with classifications of normal, near-normal, and dysplastic being used. Near the conclusion of the study, the dogs were killed, skinned, the pelves dissected, and observations made. All the dogs had nearly matured, were healthy, and none were extremely thin or fat. Their body types and skeletal structures were similar. A "pelvic muscle mass index" was calculated for each dog, being the ratio of the weight of the pelvic muscles to the total body weight. Stated another way, the index is the percentage of a dog's weight which is found in the pelvic muscles.

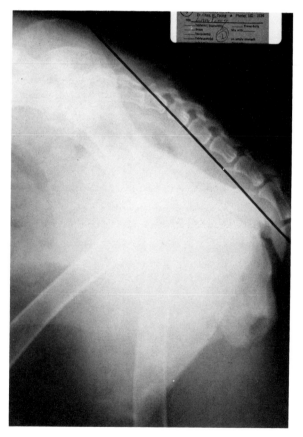

Fig. 6-5. Croup angle of German Shepherd bitch shown while standing in a "show pose."

The Greyhound had a much larger pelvic muscle mass compared with the German Shepherd Dog, which in turn had a greater amount of pelvic muscle than did the July Foxhound. Bone size and shape, including pelvic angle, were similar, indicating the importance of muscle mass as a factor. It was found that above a pelvic muscle mass index of 10.9 hip dysplasia almost never occurs, while below an index of 9.0 dysplasia always occurs. The range of indexes in the German Shepherd Dogs was wide in two of the groups, especially the dysplastic ones, and an overlap existed, but the mean index was always lower as the degree of dysplasia increased.

Group 1 consisted of Greyhounds, approximately one third of which had never raced or received training, and none of this group was in racing condition at the time of the study.

Group 2 consisted of seven German Shepherd Dogs, six of which had received training for sentry or guide work. Group 3 also consisted of German Shepherd Dogs originally selected for breeding but culled because of poor temperament. All had normal or near-normal hips. Group 4 was a large group of German Shepherd Dogs, all dysplastic. Groups 5 and 6 were July Foxhounds which were kennel-raised and badly dysplastic (subluxated) to severely dysplastic (luxated) by the time they were six months old.

The question has been raised whether pelvic muscle mass is inherited or acquired through roadwork or training. Of course, conditioning is helpful in firming or "toning up" muscles, but it has been my experience that the animal either has it or it doesn't.

In many years as a professional handler, I had observed and shown dogs which had spent most of their lives in crates and small kennel runs, yet had beautifully muscular thighs and shoulders

TABLE IV. DOGS GROUPED BY DEGREE OF HIP DYSPLASIA.

| Group | Hip Joints | Muscle Mass Index | | |
		minimum	mean	maximum
1. Greyhounds	normal	11.7	14.2	16.3
2. Shepherds	normal	10.3	11.4	13.2
3. Shepherds	near-normal	10.3	11.0	11.4
4. Shepherds	dysplastic	5.2	9.0	12.0
5. July Hounds	subluxated	7.4	7.9	8.5
6. July Hounds	luxated	4.4	5.6	6.5

and loins compared with the free-running family pets we usually beat for the ribbons. Had those clients of mine given their dogs more exercise, an even greater difference may have been noticed, and a few more purple ribbons might have been ours.

TABLE V. EXPECTED INCIDENCE OF HIP DYSPLASIA.
(according to Dr. Wayne Riser)

Index	Comments
14.20	All dogs have normal hips; disease unreported.
12.17	All dogs have normal hips, but HD reported in some siblings.
11.63	94 percent probability these dogs would have normal hips.
10.89	86 percent probability these dogs would have normal hips.
9.00	All dogs have some degree of dysplasia.
8.00	All dogs have badly dysplastic hip joints.
5.60	All dogs have luxated hip joints.

The pelvic muscle study[70,73] reached the same conclusions in a more scientific way: one of the Greyhounds in Group 1 was confined to a cage about a cubic meter in size, yet had an index of 14.9, which is greater than the mean for that group. Two of the German Shepherd Dogs which had gone through rigorous training in the Armed Forces program had higher indexes than the average for German Shepherd Dogs with normal hips, but lower than the range in the Greyhounds which had received *no* training.

Besides differences in mass of the pelvic muscles, the fascia (layer of tissue coating the other muscle tissues) was thicker and heavier in the Greyhound than in the other two breeds, and the tendons and ligaments were larger and coarser. Almost no fat was found in the fascia or under the skin of the Greyhounds, including those pen- or cage-raised. Since training and exercise were not influencing factors, inheritance contributes everything to tissue structure, muscle mass, and hence the occurrence of normal hips.

It has been said[71] that hip dysplasia can be controlled by increasing the pelvic muscle mass. But since an accurate measurement of an individual's pelvic muscle mass index can only be obtained after dissection, and sperm banks for dogs are not commercially feasible, it may be better stated that high muscle mass ratios *and* better hips can be obtained by selectively breeding those individuals which have the best radiographs and body structure.

SECTION II
Growth
and Development
of the Canine
Hip Joint

Chapter 7
Development of
the Normal Hip

The life of a new individual begins when a sperm cell penetrates an egg cell, later to divide over and over again into a multitude of different tissues, organs, and systems. All the "blueprints" for every one of that individual's cells are present in the genes—those sub-microscopic chemical packets of inheritance information on the chromosomes.

Very early in the embryo's formation, complete structures develop, although not necessarily radiographically visible in part or entirety. Removal of the embryo from the womb once was required to see this, but today there are instruments capable of transmitting a view of the growing fetus by fiber optics and allied means.

The hip joint of the embryonic puppy is composed of cartilage, which chemically is mostly water and long-chain organic molecules of a complex starch- or sugar-like structure. Even at birth, there is next to no minerals or collagen in the joint. In the area of this primitive joint are two simple bone shapes which are later to become parts of the pelvis, and a slightly longer bone which will later take on the characteristic shape of the femur.

In the embryologic state, a single cartilaginous cap covers the top or proximal end of the femur. As muscles develop, they pull and separate that end into two main features, the greater trochanter and the head of the femur, both remaining cartilage until some time after birth and further growth. Nevertheless, whatever the biochemical makeup at any stage of growth before or after birth, the femur/acetabulum hip joint is a functional, articulating structure. The closer it gets to full maturation, the more resistant a normal hip gets to the forces of environment.

It has been said that the hip joints of all dogs are normal at time of birth.[54,70] Perhaps it would be more accurate to add "as far as we can tell." Normal structure is best evidenced by radiography, as was indicated in Chapter 1.

But can one see the complete structures of the hip assembly on a radiograph taken at birth or shortly thereafter? No. Some X-rays pass through dense material such as bone, but many are absorbed and don't reach the photographic film in the cassette. The radiation passes much more easily through the softer tissues such as cartilage and muscle, thus exposing the film to a much greater extent. Since the development of the skeleton is not complete until much later, radiographs of very young pups cannot show the entire joint; so *much* of the cartilage or other connective tissue will not yet have turned into bone. The extremely dysplastic hip can sometimes be detected radiographically by 8 to 12 weeks of age, but most dysplastic hips can only be distinguished from normal ones on radiographs after the pup is 20 weeks old.[68]

At birth, the entire joint is there, including the acetabular socket as well as the bones, but only the center portions of the ilium and ischium are visible, the rest being radiolucent cartilage. As the pup grows, the cartilaginous ends of these bones ossify progressively outward, away from the bones' centers. The thickness also increases in the same manner, but the most dramatic change takes place at the epiphyses and metaphyses adjoining the growth plates (see Fig. 15-1 in Chapter 15).

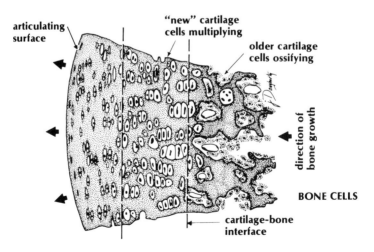

Fig. 7-1. Oversimplified representation of the end of a limb with cartilage covering the growing surface. Example—femoral head. Of course, similar growth takes place transversely, to make bones wider and thicker as well as longer.

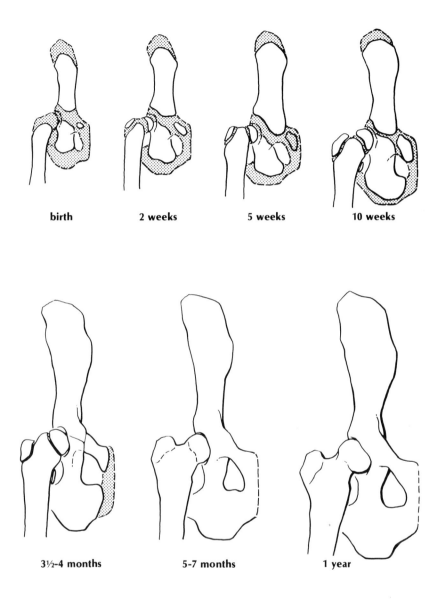

birth   2 weeks   5 weeks   10 weeks

3½-4 months   5-7 months   1 year

Fig. 7-2. Development of the normal hip. Only bone tissue shows up well on radiographs, but the entire hip structure is there nevertheless. Cartilage femoral heads, cartilage sockets, gradually ossify. At about seven months of age, growth tapers off from its steep curve and very little further change from cartilage to bone takes place. The dog is now almost at its full skeletal size. Congruity is maintained throughout growth, and can be demonstrated by palpation, radiography, and dissection. (See Fig. 8-1 in Chapter 8 for comparison with a dysplastic joint.)

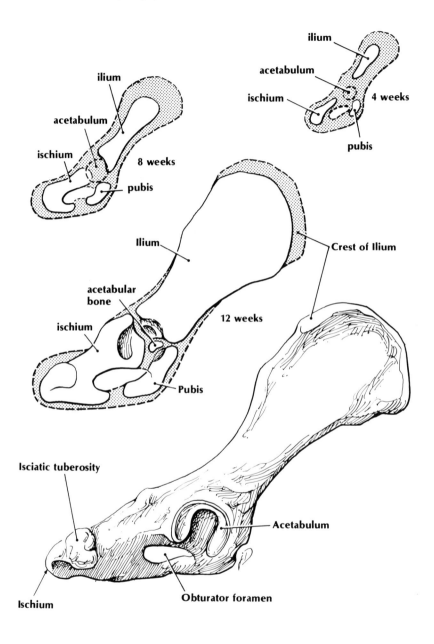

Fig. 7-3. Development of right hip, viewed from the right side (lateral aspect). Dotted lines indicate cartilage. Note entire hip is present since before birth, but ossification of cartilage takes about 10 months from conception to skeletal maturity. Solid lines indicate bone.

Growth of the Pelvis

By about four weeks of age a small projection of bone appears on the "top inside" (cranial) edge of each ischium, and what is to become the pubic bone starts taking shape. This pubis unites with its corresponding half at the center at around nine weeks, and by the eleventh to fourteenth week combines with the curved opposite (caudal) end of the ischium, which also has been growing all the while. The union of pubis and ischium forms a circle called the obturator foramen, the oval "hole" in each side of the hip through which pass nerves, blood vessels, and certain muscles.

While the ischium's caudal (rearmost) tuberosity can be easily felt by the dog owner, being the two prominences astride the tail in the area of the vulva or anus, and are the two "bones" one sits on, the pubis is not so easily palpated. In the human, one can readily find the pubic ridge below the abdomen and above the genitals.

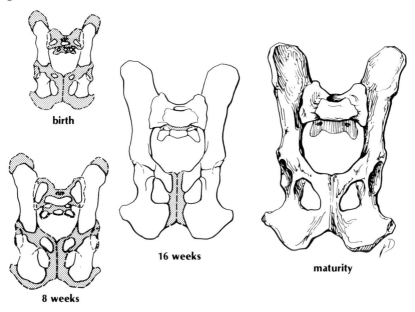

birth

8 weeks

16 weeks

maturity

Fig. 7-4. Ossification and growth of the pelvis, composed of the ilium on top, the ischium below it, and the pubis to the front. They encircle the acetabular bone, forming the acetabulum or hip socket. The two ilium bones, right and left, meet at the fused vertebrae known as the sacrum, at an angle which remains fairly constant from birth to maturity.

The third major bone of the pelvic girdle is the ilium, with a scapula-like wing on top (the cranial end). The highest prominences of this pair are those felt when passing the hand along the dog's topline from back and loin to the croup and tail (*See* Figs. 1-1 and 7-3). Halfway from that crest to the acetabulum, and on the medial or inside edge, this ilium is joined to the spine by cartilage and ligaments, becoming fused later. The bones of the sacrum, which are the vertebrae of the spine at that junction, also fuse and cannot flex as can the rest of the spine or tail.

Neither the croup angle (slope of sacrum in relation to the ilium) nor the 3:2 length ratio of ilium to ischium changes visibly during the whole growth period.

One more bone makes up the hip-bone assembly: the acetabular bone, a very small piece which with the ends of the ilium, ischium, and pubis form the acetabulum or "hip socket." The fusion of those bones cannot early be observed radiologically because the head of the femur, which is relatively thick, tends to

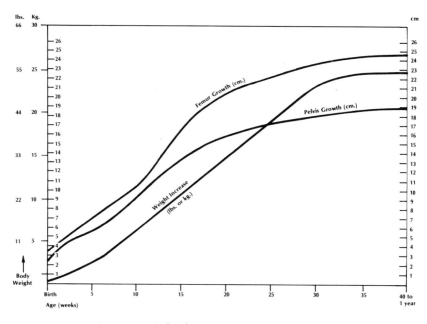

Fig. 7-5. Rate of growth of the hip joint and allied bones. Growth patterns of the combined pelvic bones (os coxae) and femurs are similar. Fastest skeletal growth is between 9 and 27 weeks of age. This figure is based on a study of track Greyhounds, and a different weight curve may be seen in other breeds.

hide their development until the acetabulum has sufficiently ossified. This happens by about the third month after birth.

Until the pelvic bones have reached maturity, have stopped growing, and have united to form one contiguous structure, the separate parts were held together and in place by cartilaginous growth plates called physes. These are indicated on some of the accompanying figures. Such growth plates are made up of columns of cartilage cells lined up at right angles to the borders of the bones, and in some joints these columns are several layers thick. Those cells on the end furthest from the main portion of the bone multiply, pushing some toward the bone and extending the length of the unit. As these cartilage cells reach the other end of the growth plate (closest to the bone) they become calcified and turn into bone. This is the process of ossification, specifically endochondral (from cartilage) ossification. (see Fig. 7-1).

Now, when two such growth areas meet, there is nowhere for the cells furthest from each bone to go, and bone formation keeps closing the gap until there is no more cartilage left; all has calcified and bone cells have filled all the changed cartilage cells. Two bones have become one. In the skull, many of these bones take quite a while to unite, otherwise the adult's head would be hardly bigger than the newborn's. Who hasn't seen and felt the "soft spot" on a human baby's cranium?

In the case of joints, a layer of connective tissue remains to keep the bones from uniting and thereby preventing articulation. If the joint is defective, such tissue can be worn away in one area, permitting bone-to-bone abrasion and polished (eburnated) surfaces, and can stimulate abnormal connective tissue and bone growth on other adjacent areas.

Growth of the Femur

In a study of track Greyhounds which were raised and examined in order to determine the histological* development of normal vs. dysplastic hips, measurements were taken of the length of the femur and other bones by tracing many radiographs of dogs at various intervals during growth.[69] Because only the main part of the shaft is formed as bone by time of birth, the cartilaginous ends being radiolucent, it was difficult to measure the entire length of tissues which would later be all bone. Some of the line drawings

---

*Dealing with the microscopic study of the structure of tissues.

in this chapter represent only the radiopaque portions, not the surrounding cartilage or other soft tissues. By two weeks after birth the ends of the femur become visible.

The femur grows at a uniform rate, correlating with the growth (by weight) curve of the dog, with the greatest slope being between the tenth and thirtieth weeks. The femur attains 95 percent of the adult length in most breeds by seven months of age, with only about a tenth of a centimeter to go to reach the maximum. The shape of the femur evidences a head and condyles (knobs on the bottom) by about two weeks, and by four or five weeks the small bony end attaches to the top of the shaft, with a double line on the sketch of the radiograph representing the growth plate. The round head at the top of the femur develops a small notch or fossa at about seven or eight weeks where the teres ligament is attached, its other attachment being at the center of the acetabulum.

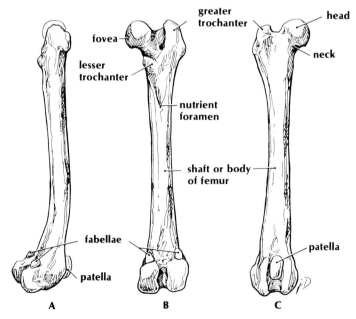

Fig. 7-6. The femur.
A—Right femur in place, viewed from the side (lateral view).
B—Right femur viewed from the rear (caudal aspect). Seed-shaped sesamoid bones are incidental to this study, but their presence is often obvious on radiographs. Note fovea on head. This is where teres ligament is inserted; it will appear as a flat spot on some radiographs, depending upon rotation of femur.
C—Right femur viewed from the front (cranial aspect).

There are three growth plates in the femur: one at the lower end and one at the top end, which latter separates into two as the greater trochanter (a shoulder- or ridge-type structure) moves away and becomes distinct from the head. The columns of cartilage in these growth plates change in a continuous process of bone deposition and resorption, with the "bottom" line of bone cells in the *head*, for example, being destroyed and replaced by the top layer of cartilage cells covering the *shaft*, thus allowing the shaft to also grow in length instead of all the growth taking place in the head. Those new cartilage cells in turn multiply, are pushed toward the body of the femur, and are changed into the bone cells of the femur. By five months of age, 80 percent of the ossification (bone formation from cartilage and such connective tissue) has been completed, and the growth plate narrows and finally disappears by age 12 to 14 months. The above changes are the reasons why very few dogs beyond seven months of age exhibit their

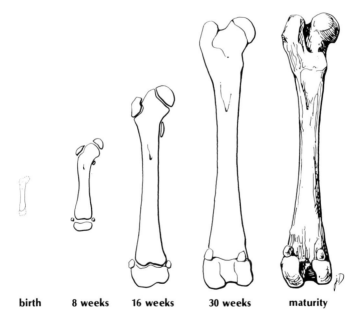

| birth | 8 weeks | 16 weeks | 30 weeks | maturity |

Fig. 7-7. Growth of the femur. The dot about two-thirds up the shaft is the nutrient foramen, where a major blood vessel enters the marrow. It serves as a reference point in measuring growth of the upper and lower segments of the femur.

first signs of dysplasia, and indicate that if a dog gets through this period of its life without clinical signs, it may not, depending on amount of work, show evidence again until several years later when the secondary degeneration (arthritis) becomes a source of pain.

As the muscles of the pelvis develop, the trochanter is pulled away from the head, and a depression called the trochanteric fossa is formed, wherein other muscles are attached. This pulling and shaping of bone by muscle is a normal part of development. It is a surprise to many who find out that seemingly rigid, immovable bone is actually plastic, deformable tissue which is shaped by the pull of muscles over a long and perhaps steady period. In the dysplastic hip, abnormal change in shape is called remodelling.

By the time the acetabular rim has ossified enough to be visible on a radiograph, the three-month old pup has been running, playing, and putting considerable stresses on these still-forming tissues of the hip joint. This cavity, the acetabulum, is one of the key structures in the study of hip dysplasia. Even when the femoral

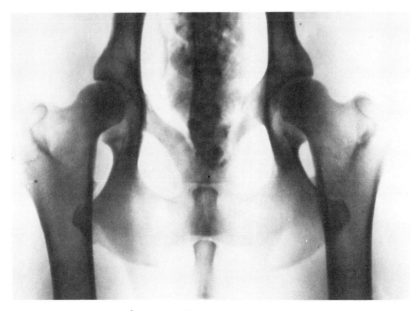

Fig. 7-8. Normal hips. Lladnek's Billie Bonnie.
Courtesy of Ed Rymsa and Bill Richards, Jr.
Rym-Sas Kennels

head could only be described radiographically as an opaque dot at less than two weeks, it was positioned well within the cavity, and in the normal hip, approximately two-thirds of the head remains within the acetabulum during mineralization (calcification, ossification). Hip joints continue to develop normally as long as such congruity is maintained.

Chapter 8
Development of
the Dysplastic Hip

In an earlier chapter we have examined or briefly presented a wide variety of theories on the cause or causes of hip dysplasia. In subsequent chapters treatment and control will be discussed, but in the present chapter the radiologic development of the "typical" dysplastic hip, if there could be any such thing as that, is outlined. Hip dysplasia has been seen as a genetic disease characterized by too-rapid skeletal growth and relatively insufficient muscle mass, and the canine hip has been reported to be normal at birth. Joint instability is a result of the failure of muscle to mature at the same rate as the skeleton,[61,70] and to hold the femoral head in the ace-tabulum (socket). Hip dysplasia and secondary degenerative joint disease occur primarily as the result of insufficient strength of the soft tissues to maintain the necessary congruity or stability of the joint that we mentioned in Chapter 7.

Paralleling Riser's work with normal Greyhounds was his study of dysplasia in German Shepherd Dogs.[72] These were from a col-ony expected to produce dysplastic individuals, and all were handled the same way as the group of Greyhounds in Chapter 7. Hip dysplasia varied from mild to severe, with palpable and radi-ographic evidence ranging from seven weeks to more than a year of age. Four of the Shepherds were radiographed weekly from birth to maturity, and radiographic tracings were made of the hip of one of these, which was representative of the other three.

From birth to about one month of age, some 87 dogs were dissected, and their appearance at this young age were similar to that of the Greyhounds in 84 of the cases. In the other three, some damage to the teres ligament was seen as the earliest evi-dence of hip dysplasia. And this at an age when locomotion has been a new experience! During the first 30 days, the teres liga-ment is responsible for holding the femoral head in place, but by the time a dysplastic dog has matured, the teres ligament can stretch enough so that the head subluxes to the edge of the acetabulum.

In the more severe cases, hip dysplasia can be recognized radiographically at age eight weeks. Laxity can sometimes be palpated at this age, too. (*See* Chapter 13 for a description of such palpation.) The acetabular rim does not develop at a normal rate, and no longer has a clean, sharp edge. The teres ligament has lengthened slightly, and the joint capsule appears stretched. Between two and three months of age, dramatic changes occur. In the German Shepherd Dogs of this study, subluxation increased, and in the euthanized and dissected dogs, the capsules were so thickened and stretched that the heads could be moved out to the edges of the acetabula. The teres ligament was typically swollen, and the cartilage on the femoral head showed signs of wear. Also by three months, the greater trochanter was bent by the tension of some of the gluteal muscles, the greater-than-usual pull being the result of the head being displaced medially (toward the middle axis of the dog).

The changes just described happen as well in other structures, not just bone and cartilage. While they may be described[70] as "cartilaginous drift," accomplished by "fatigue-bending," the process is similar to a condition in the field of materials testing known as "creep," a slow deformation or slide produced by a steady force. Fatigue is one such mode of deformation, with possible fracture, produced by repeated stress, such as impact, for example. The elastic limit, that point at which a material has been permanently deformed, is reached in ligament and especially bone structures of the dysplastic hip. New bone formation takes place to fill some of the voids created by the drifting growth plate in the femoral head, and bone is resorbed in other nearby locations. Both osseous (bone) drift and cartilage (growth plate) drift occur, and tissues are more susceptible to microscopic fracture.

During the period from 12 to 20 weeks of age, the components of the joint continue to change shape, and the acetabular rim rolls back even further. The degree to which congruity is disrupted varies with the severity of the disease in the individual. Most of the changes described here are more easily seen upon dissection and histological study than on radiographs.

From 20 weeks (four and one-half months) to about eight and one-half months the head of the femur begins to take on the appearance of a rivet or a well-used tent stake, or perhaps the analogy of a railroad spike is better, since the drift is more toward

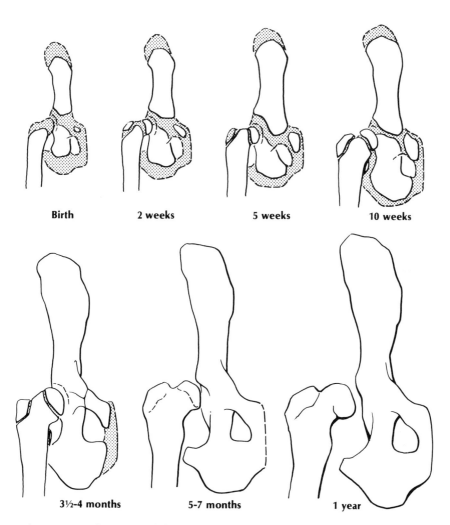

Birth   **2 weeks**   **5 weeks**   **10 weeks**

3½-4 months   **5-7 months**   **1 year**

Fig. 8-1. Development of the dysplastic hip. While there are many levels of severity, and considerable differences between individuals, the above drawings indicate the progression of HD in a fairly severe case. Between 2 and 3 months of age, sometimes as early as 7 weeks, an abnormal development of the acetabular rim can be seen on radiography. The femoral head is subluxated, the stretched teres ligament allows a poor fit into a shallow acetabulum, and ossification of the acetabular rim is slower than in a normal hip. The greater trochanter is bent toward the pelvis, bone fills the "valley" between trochanter and femoral head, the head becomes flattened and lipped over, and the head rests on the far outside rim of the acetabulum. The deeper part of the acetabulum fills with new bone to take up unused space. (see Fig. 7-2 for comparison with normal hip development.)

one side. The edge rolls over like a dip of ice cream pushed too hard into the cone. The joint capsule, meanwhile, has thickened considerably and hip motion and length of stride become restricted—a normal arc of 110 degrees may be reduced to only 45 degrees, even with the help of anesthesia. The synovial (joint) fluid no longer functions as a lubricant, the teres ligament may rupture, and other ligaments swell so much that the head cannot fit back into the now shallow acetabulum. The fossa of the acetabulum begins to fill with a fibrous bone.

Such remodelling and degeneration progresses at an even greater rate after the age of eight and one-half or nine months, and it becomes difficult to say which changes are due to the dysplasia and which to the secondary degenerative disease. Even other, non-articulating surfaces of the pelvic bones show roughening and distortion as a result of excessive forces tending to tear the gluteal muscles away and bringing about a form of osseous drift there, too.

To review what has already been covered in Chapter 1 in the light of the more thorough description just above, this is how the disease proceeds: at first, very little if any pain is exhibited by most pups even with the most severe cases of HD. Then, perhaps at age five or six months a pup may suddenly show signs of pain after exercise, arising, climbing, or jumping. The pain is likely due to the microfractures of the acetabular rim, even though they are similar to a condition which in humans has been commonly termed a "hairline fracture." Healing of the microfractures usually takes place as the pup nears 90 percent of its adult size, between its eighth and eleventh months, and the pain susbides. Most dysplastic dogs rise and walk without pain at 11 to 13 months of age.

At this point, the dog may show no pain with moderate exercise, but the gait may be affected, especially as the dog nears a point of exhaustion from trotting or other work. Often, it is not noticed, because the dog does not swing its legs in a greater-than-45° arc when walking. Better correlation between clinical and radiographic signs can be had if the dog is worked hard, or if the degree of dysplasia is great, or if the individual has a relatively low pain threshold.

The conclusions of Riser's work with the dysplastic German Shepherd Dogs were that hip dysplasia occurs if congruity of femoral head and acetabulum is not maintained until ossification is complete and the supporting soft tissues become strong enough to prevent subluxation.

SECTION III
Control
of Hip Dysplasia
in the Individual

Chapter 9
Treatment of
the Dysplastic Dog

by Wayne H. Riser, D.V.M.

(Author's note: I am deeply indebted and thankful to Dr. Wayne Riser for contributing this chapter on treatment for my book. Inasmuch as it was originally intended for a professional readership, I have added a glossary at the end for the benefit of the lay reader.)

There is no successful method of treatment for canine hip dysplasia that will restore total normal function. Well over 50 percent of the dogs larger in size than the ancestral dog are affected, but few are worked to the point where they actually need treatment. In addition, many owners are not aware that their individual dogs are affected and these dogs do not need treatment. This is true even for the dogs that are shown or entered in obedience trials, unless their training is prolonged for long hours on a daily basis.

Some dogs are restricted clinically by hip dysplasia and the accompanying degenerative joint disease of the hips and would be more comfortable if under treatment. Some affected dogs worked hard on a daily basis for tracking, police work, and retrieving and jumping perform subnormally and hold back because of fatigue and soreness. Most training organizations discourage using dysplastic dogs in their work. A few dogs suffer intensely and are worthless cripples without treatment. It is rare, however, when some measure of benefit cannot be given to any dogs crippled with hip dysplasia. A number of possibilities are available for the relief of pain and the improvement of locomotion.

Hip dysplasia is usually bilateral (93 percent) and the clinically affected dogs fall into two groups: 1) the young dogs (five to eight months), and 2) the mature dogs (one to ten years of age) who are chronically affected. These two groups of dogs are handled and treated differently because the nature of the pain and disability are different.

Younger Dogs

In the young dogs, there are sudden signs of difficult rising, running, and stair climbing associated with marked soreness of the hind limbs. Subluxation of the femoral heads is the chief and perhaps the only radiographic finding. The conformation of the femoral heads at this point appear normal; if, however, the process has been present for several months, the angle of the femoral necks may be more valgus (over 135 degrees), or there may be ventral drifting of the epiphyses causing lipping of the ventral aspect. The acetabulums appear larger than the femoral heads, and the anterio-dorsal acetabular rims reveal varying degrees of underdevelopment and later remodelling.

The sudden and prolonged pain and crippling locomotion in the young dog is the result of sudden occurrence of microfractures of the acetabular rims between the "ten and two o'clock positions." These fractures are not visible radiographically because they are hidden behind the femoral heads and occur as a result of prolonged fatigue and bending of the immature bone of the acetabular rims caused by the forces of the body weight and motion upon the part.

The events leading up to microfracture formation are interesting and worth noting. In the normal hip, the forces from body weight and motion of the joint are distributed over the entire articular surface of the horse-shoe configuration of the acetabulums and the femoral heads. But when the femoral heads are subluxated, only a small area of the articular surfaces of both femoral heads and the acetabulums contact each other. Such limited contact produces concentrated stresses and forces in a small area on the dorsal rims between the ten and two o'clock positions. Continual bending and overloading of the rim produces fatigue, loss of tissue elasticity, contour, and eventual fracture. Pain results from tension on and tearing of the nerves of the periosteum. Once the fractures have occurred on the anterio-dorsal rims, the acetabular sockets lose their curvature (contour) and straighten. The frayed ends of the rim turn upward and backward. Sharpey's fibers (the attachment between bone and muscles, tendons, and ligaments) rupture, bleed, and form osteophytes.

These osseous projections of new bone build up around the acetabulums and become radiographically visible around the seventeenth month of age. Before this much time has elapsed, the healing of the microfractures has occurred, which is usually by the time the growth plates close (11 to 13 months), the pelvis is fully ossified, and the hip joints become stable and usually pain-free. Most dysplastic dogs at 12 to 14 months of age, regardless of the degree of hip dysplasia, walk and run soundly and without pain. Treatment of any kind need not be considered at this time; the hips of all young dogs stabilize at this time.

Older Dogs

The second group of dysplastic dogs that are brought in for care is the older group (1½ to 10 years or older), and these dogs are suffering from painful, chronic, degenerative joint disease. The lameness occurs in one or both hips but is usually bilateral. The signs of lameness often appear acutely after a brisk run or prolonged exercise and is the result of a local tear or injury to the abnormal tissue, but the primary cause is the chronic, long-time build-up of the degenerative joint disease and the stress applied that exceeds the reserve threshold causing a breakdown. Microfractures do not occur in the older group of dogs. Occasionally, injury to stifle ligaments occurs when a dog tries to protect a hip and overextends the joint below.

In the chronically affected hip the capsule is markedly thickened from a normal or "paper" thinness to an increase of one or more centimeters. With this increase, there is a gradual shortening of the stride. (In the normal anesthetized dog the range of motion is 110 degrees while in the chronically dysplastic dog it is reduced to as little as 45 degrees because of the thickened capsule.)

Because of discomfort and pain the dog sits rather than stands when it stops. When it rises, it does so slowly and with much difficulty. The animal may also be reluctant to chase a ball, jump, or run a long distance. The thigh muscles atrophy markedly when pain has restricted their use for weeks, months, or even years. At the same time, the shoulder muscles hypertrophy because of the cranial shift of weight and increased use of the forelimbs.

Abnormal remodelling and hypertrophic osseous development are continually progressive in and around the dysplastic hip. The key to treating such an affected dog is to restrict exercise to below the threshold level (the stress the hip joints can take without clinical signs of pain and fatigue). Most non-working dogs (pets) stay within this level and will stop and rest when pain and fatigue are felt. There may or may not be a correlation between the radiographic appearance of the hip joints and the clinical signs manifested by the dog.

Treatments

Four methods of treatment have been practiced: 1) pectinotomy, 2) femoral head removal, 3) total hip replacement, and 4) medication. The first two surgical procedures have proven beneficial, and with study, new design and materials, the third may eventually be recommended. Medication in the hands of a sympathetic veterinarian is highly recommended.

Pectinotomy on the side or sides of the crippling hip has been practiced extensively, and analysis of the results are rather controversial. The operation in no way improves the lesion of hip dysplasia. In the hands of some, results have been reported as uniformly beneficial; for others, the operation has helped temporarily, and in some dogs the results were questionable. The muscles surrounding painful hips are irritated and in spasm. Cutting across the belly of a muscle releases the spasm of a small area, severs the hypersensitive nerves to that muscle, and changes the stress forces and lines to a small area of the hip joint. That seems to be enough change, in some instances, to bring relief from pain in a hip, especially in the young dogs. It should be remembered that a few days' rest while recovering from an anesthetic and surgery, plus the fact that most young dogs ambulate soundly when the microfractures heal may influence the results from this procedure.

A lesion was reported to have been present in the cells and fibers of this muscle. This finding has not been confirmed and no lesion has ever been found in any of the hip muscles in canine hip dysplasia. The severed muscle ends may reunite in six to eight months, but this may have been time enough to bring benefit and relief of pain. In older dogs, pectinotomy has restored some retrievers to hunting; in other instances, the operation has been of little benefit.

Removal of the femoral heads at the necks near the femurs in those dogs with extensive, painful exostoses has relieved the painful degenerative joint disease and restored useful, pain-free locomotion. After removal of the femoral head, the muscles and ligaments are securely sutured together so that a workable pseudo-joint is formed. Large dogs ambulate satisfactorily with both heads removed. However, it is a rather severe ordeal when both heads are removed at the same time. The healing takes four to seven months before the pseudo-joint is completely established. The range of motion is always restricted in the dog with the pseudo-joint (45 degrees), but painless motion is restored and some dogs return to hunting and organized sports.

Total hip prosthesis in the dog has not proved satisfactory. By one year, most implants have loosened or dislocated. Improved materials and methods may eventually prove more attractive.

A number of *medicinal agents* have proved beneficial for easing the pain of degenerative joint disease. None of the drugs improves the condition. This author [ed. note: Dr. Riser] has used two drugs extensively that have been helpful over a number of years. They are the aspirin derivatives and Meclofenamic acid (such as Arquel by Parke-Davis).

Aspirin and sodium salicylate in the mild case where there is subclinical, variable restriction, improves locomotion and the well-being of the dog. The dosage is 0.5 grains per pound divided into four to six daily doses. Enteric coated tablets are recommended because salicylates are irritating to the canine gastric mucosa.

Meclofenamic acid in daily doses of 0.5 mg. per pound of body weight has been highly beneficial, even remarkable and non-toxic, for controlling pain and improving gait. This drug allows many young dogs to move about almost normally. In the older dog that has been crippled by hip dysplasia and degenerative joint disease, Arquel has enabled them to ambulate in an acceptable manner for indefinite periods without toxic effects.

A Different Disease

Another disease, spinal cord myelopathy, affecting primarily old German Shepherd Dogs (six to ten years of age) has been mistaken for crippling hip dysplasia. The clinical signs are marked hindquarter side-to-side wobbling and hindleg weakness in an otherwise bright, alert dog. These patients are unable to climb steps or jump into an automobile. The toenails of the hind feet are extensively worn, and the dog will stand on a flexed foot for long periods. The flexed foot sometimes wears away the hair from the top of the foot. Dogs so affected retain control of the bowels and urinary bladder.

The course of the disease is downhill and is from 6 to 24 months before the animal is unable to walk; this course has not been altered by any treatment so far reported. Degenerative lesions are found in the thoracic portion of the white matter of the spinal cord tracts. The cause is not known; neither is there a suggestion of why the condition is almost entirely confined to the German Shepherd Dog breed. The reason that the condition has been confused with hip dysplasia is that most old German Shepherd Dogs have radiographic evidence of hip dysplasia.

W. H. R.

Glossary for Chapter 9

Anterio-dorsal	Refers to the front-to-top area of the acetabular rim.
Atrophy	Loss of muscle tone because of lack of exercise or nourishment.
Bilateral	Affecting both sides; specifically, both hip joints.
Enteric	Affecting the intestines.
Exostosis	An abnormal bony growth on the surface of a bone.
Hypertrophy	Opposite of atrophy; excessive development of one part, often at the expense of another (*Hyper-:* over, excessive).
Mucosa	Mucous membranes or lining of certain tissues.
Myelopathy	*Myelo-:* marrow or spinal cord; *-pathy:* disease or suffering.
Periosteum	The tough, white coating on bones, by which other organs attach.
Prosthesis	An artificial substitute for a missing part of the body.
Valgus	Usually, bowlegged. In this case, "turned outward" or greater angle.

F. L. L.

Chapter 10
Overnutrition
and Growth Rate

As a breeder and former professional handler, I have often heard an old adage of the dog show world: there are two things necessary to winning—feeding and breeding. We'll look at these aspects in that order.

Roll a boulder from the peak of a mountain and you can determine on which side it will descend. That's genetic. On the way down, it'll bounce off ledges and trees, and be steered and veered by valleys and gullies. That's environment. Once a sperm cell has united with an ovum, the eventual pup's genetic bank has already been stocked, but characteristics can be modified or hidden through diet, training, activity, and other environmental forces without changing the heritage it will pass on to succeeding generations. Much of what will follow in this chapter is summed up by saying, "Overnutrition during growth increases incidence and severity of hip dysplasia in dogs with the genetic trait for the condition."[57]

A breeding program in Sweden, begun in 1969,[32] was designed to get more information about heredity and hip dysplasia, largely because of the failure in the previous ten years of an attempt by the Swedish Kennel Club to control hip dysplasia in German Shepherd Dogs by breeding methods. One reason for the failure may have been insufficient knowledge of what constituted genetic hip dysplasia, and another may have been diet: in 1959 commercial dog food was not widely used in Europe, but by the late 60's it was the main food supply for kennels. "Better" nutrition and more intense feeding of puppies in the rapid growth period between two and six months of age are said[58] to have possibly counterbalanced the attempted genetic selection.

In the 1950's the discovery was made that most large dogs had hip dysplasia.[71] A survey and analysis of the existing literature led to the following conclusions:

1. Most large breeds are affected, and there is a correlation between hip dysplasia and size;

2. Hip dysplasia is seldom a problem in dogs with a mature weight of under 25 pounds, especially in those with short legs;[67]

3. The American racing Greyhound is apparently genetically free of hip dysplasia, and Greyhounds in this category have from 50 to 100 percent more pelvic muscle mass than German Shepherd Dogs, regardless of exercise;

4. Dogs' hips are apparently normal at birth, and signs of dysplasia appear beginning at 8 to 20 weeks, with the highest incidence related to rapid growth rate and early weight gain, and the lowest environmentally controlled incidence related to confinement which kept weight off the hips;

5. Hip dysplasia is polygenic and not sex-linked; that is, the genes are not located on the sex chromosomes;

6. Incidence and severity can be reduced by careful selection of breeding partners; and

7. Hip dysplasia is common to many domesticated species and man, but not wild animals; thus, it may be a man-made condition.

Some of these points will be reviewed later in Section IV, but for now let's concentrate on points one, two, four, and seven above.

Size

Through the years of selecting for certain desirable traits such as a formidable appearance for guard dogs, a large frame for freighting dogs which are expected to pull wagons or heavy sleds, or just an impressive show dog, breeders have increased the size of most breeds. If lap dogs or racing dogs such as the Whippet, which has a maximum-height or disqualification to watch out for in its standard, truly have a lower incidence of dysplasia than the larger breeds, it may be partly because of a tendency not to increase the size of the breed in question.

On the other hand, people are impressed by a BIG Saint or Mastiff or Golden or whatever, and pay higher prices for them than they would for their smaller littermates. Following generations then are not only selectively *bred* for size, they are also *fed* for maximum size. Individuals with the genetic potential and early joint laxity are being overloaded with weight because they are being overfed as early as they are weaned. Result: more stress on less-than-perfect hips and subsequent degeneration of the coxo-femoral joints. Most of the damage is done while much of the acetabular rim is still in the process of changing from cartilage to bone.

It has been found that dogs less than a foot tall at the withers and less than 25 pounds in weight, such as the Dachshund, are relatively free of hip dysplasia. On the other hand, at least half the larger dogs weighing over 75 pounds and standing over 20 inches at the shoulders are affected by hip dysplasia.[71] Note the word "relatively." Hip dysplasia has been found in toy breeds but, because of their light weight, the biomechanical stresses are generally inconsequential. There are always exceptions to general rules: Beagles have a fairly high percentage of hip dysplasia, according to records kept or observations made on this breed which is a popular choice for laboratory study.[68]

Early Weight Gain

Puppies which have suffered setbacks because of coccidiosis, worms, virus infections, or other health problems usually have better hip joint development than their faster-growing, apparently healthier siblings or other litters. It is generally felt that this is due to less weight on the acetabula and supporting tissues during formation, so laxity either did not occur or did not affect the shapes of the bones and other tissues in the joint capsule. It was found in one study on German Shepherd Dogs[71] that there were no pups weighing over 20 pounds at 60 days of age that didn't develop hip dysplasia. While there are exceptions, it's a pretty good rule of thumb. I owned one of those exceptions, a German Shepherd Dog that weighed more than 20 pounds at eight weeks, with hips that OFA classified as normal at age four years, and which at 13 years had no trouble with his hips nor any special diet of supplements. But remember the generality is never disproven by the exception. Thin puppies, like thin humans, are healthier as a rule.

Rate of maturation (time to reach adult size) is another factor more related to genetics, which will be discussed later, but it is possible to accelerate it by overnutrition in the individual dog. Today's commercial dog foods are richer in all nutrients known to be needed by dogs than were the preparations of the earlier half of the century. Dogs then may have received enough protein, fat, and carbohydrate from their meat and table scraps diet, but likely the vitamins, trace minerals, and balance of nutrients were not as "good," nor was palatability as high in most cases. Present offerings are tasty and encourage hearty appetites; thus, today's dog may eat more. You know that if your food is bland you'll be less likely to reach for second helpings. People who change jobs and go on expense accounts always seem to gain weight. Perhaps this is because they now have a wider choice of tastier food, and it's "ad libitum."

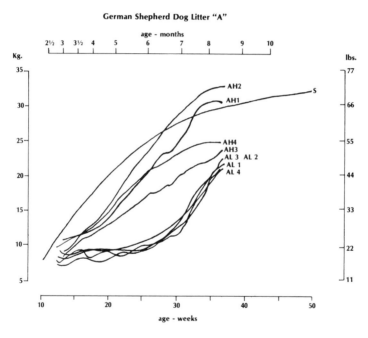

Fig. 10-1. **Effect of growth rate. Both parents of "A" litter were dysplastic, most of the pups had positive indication of hip dysplasia by palpation (both Ortolani and Bardens techniques), yet all were radiographically normal at age 37 weeks. Only two of the "A" litter had exceeded the Purina standard weight curves, and then only briefly before the experiment ended. Other litters had growth rates equal to, over, or close to the standard growth curve for their breeds and each had a high proportion of severe hip dysplasia. As in the case of litter "A," parents were dysplastic. Therefore we see that it is possible to prevent dysplasia in a genetically predisposed individual.**

The following radiographs compare the hips of dogs in three litters: A, B, and E, identified as to method of feeding (H=high caloric intake, L=lower relative intake of food). This shows that HD can become rapidly worse, and slow weight gain may not be enough to prevent the progression.

Reprinted from "Nutrition, Weight Gain, and Development of Hip Dysplasia," by Hakan Kasstrom. Department of Clinical Radiology, the Royal Veterinary College, Stockholm, Sweden, and the Laboratory for Comparative Orthopaedics, The Hospital for Special Surgery, affiliated with the Cornell University Medical College, New York, 1975.

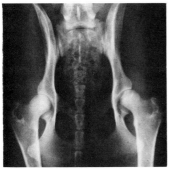 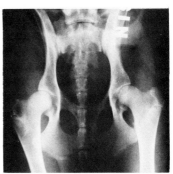

Figure 10-2. Dog AH3, 37 weeks of age. Normal hip joints.   **Fig. 10-3. Dog AL3, 37 weeks of age. Normal hip joints.**

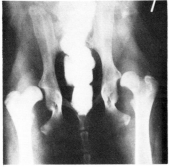 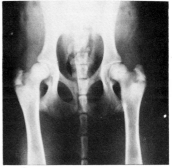

Fig. 10-4. Dog BH2, 33 weeks of age. Hip dysplasia grade IV.   **Fig. 10-5. Dog BL2, 33 weeks of age. Normal hip joints.**

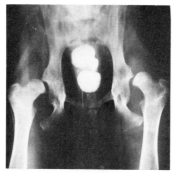

Fig. 10-6. Dog BH3, 33 weeks of age. Hip dysplasia grade IV

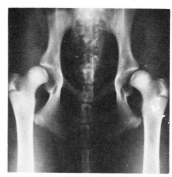

Fig. 10-7. Dog BL3, 33 weeks of age. Hip dysplasia grade III.

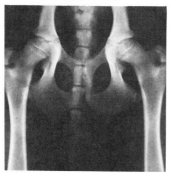

Fig. 10-8. Dog EH1, 27 weeks of age. Hip dysplasia grade III.

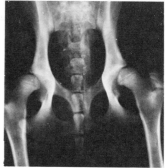

Fig. 10-9. Dog EH1, 22 weeks of age. Normal hip joints.

The 1974 Cornell Study

In an experimental study of growing Great Danes culminating early in 1974 at Cornell,[30] researchers made some important discoveries on nutrition and growth. Pups in the experiment were classified into two groups: A and R. The A-dogs were fed as much as they wanted (Ad libitum) of a tasty meal twice a day, two dogs to a kennel to encourage appetite. The R-dogs (Restricted) were fed individually, and two-thirds the amount given A-dogs. Blood analyses were done, joints (feet, spine, shoulders, pelvis) were radiographed, and after necropsy, bones were studied from a large number of aspects.

A-dogs nibbled all day, while R-dogs wolfed down their meals in a minute or less. Each A-dog was "paired" with an R-dog for the purpose of studying the effects of feeding on dogs of same or very similar age, sex, birth weight, etc. Within each pair, the A-dog grew heavier in a very short time after the start of the experiment, males faster than females. The A-dogs got into the habit of just eating and resting, but spent very little time playing, in spite of having kennel mates. They walked (clumsily), rather than ran, while their smaller R counterparts were lively and ran around chasing other dogs in play.

A-dogs did not exhibit excessive fat, so the breeder or puppy owner should not take body fat as a measure of nutrition. They had a very definite enlargement of the distal end of the long bones of the front legs early in the study (knobby knees), pasterns appeared weak, and front feet tended to splay and appear "east-west." Some degree of sway-back developed, the pups became cowhocked, and bumps grew quite large at the ends of the ribs where the cartilage starts.

While young R-dogs made a game of jumping on and off a one-foot-high platform, the A-dogs of the same age refused to get down or to get their rear ends up without help. These signs, as well as a couple of instances of ataxia similar to the wobbler syndrome common in Danes and Dobermans, reached a peak early in the program, and never quite disappeared. Calcium and phosphorus levels in both groups were essentially identical in both percent of diet and in bone analysis made after death, though the A-dogs had consumed more of these minerals simply because they ate more food.

The angle made by the shaft of the femur and the neck leading to the femoral head plays a part in the transmission of forces to the acetabulum; the less the angle, the poorer the fit. A-dogs had a more obtuse angle; i.e., the neck was closer to being parallel to the femur than was the case with the R-dogs, which had a more normal angle. The condition is known as coxa valga. The femoral neck was also thickened in comparison with the R counterparts.

How this possibly comes about is too technical and detailed to appear in a book of this scope, but briefly stated, one theorized route is this: excessive food intake yields excessive calcium (among other things), to which the body responds by producing more calcitonin and less parathormone. Both calcium and gastrin (secreted in a part of the stomach called the pyloric antrum) stimulate calcitonin secretion and decrease the activity of the parathyroid glands. This seems to retard bone resorption, throwing off balance the natural growth of the joints.

Excess calcitonin and a resultant process are presumed to be instrumental not only in forming an abnormal thickness of cartilage and abnormal size of the growth plates, but in remodelling the neck of the femur as well. Proper maturation of this and other parts of the skeletal system is consequently disrupted, according to the theory.

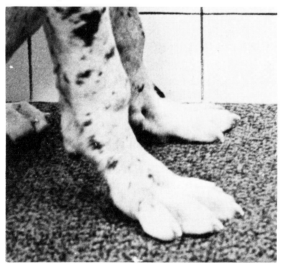

Fig. 10-10. Dog A9-1 in the Cornell study, fed at libitum, after only 3 weeks on the experiment, Note pronounced widening of the metaphysis of distal radius and ulna (wrist), and the sinking of the metacarpo-phalangeal joints (pastern and toes).

Courtesy of Dr. Lennart Krook, New York
State College of Veterinary Medicine

Whether related to any inherited aggressiveness in nursing or other genetic or environmental aspects, some dogs will gain weight more rapidly than others. An experiment[74] involving 222 German Shepherd Dogs showed a definite correlation between hip dysplasia at one year and their weights at 60 days of age. The heavier pups at two months had the higher incidence of hip dysplasia as a group. One hundred of the pups were dysplastic at one year, and their mean weight at two months was 14 pounds, while the 122 diagnosed at one year to be normal had, as 60-day-old pups, a mean weight of 13 pounds. This difference of 4 percent was deemed significant, and despite the averages, only about a third of the dysplastic dogs had been under the average weight, and only five of the 122 normal dogs were over. The dysplastic males had averaged 14½ pounds compared to the normal males at 13.4 pounds. Dysplastic females were 13.8 pounds and normal females 12.3 pounds. This doesn't mean that your 14½ pound two-month male pup is going to be dysplastic, and your neighbor's

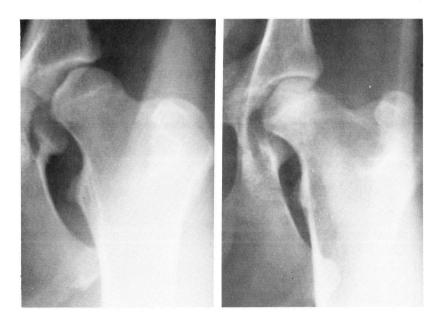

Fig. 10-11. Dog A48-1 and R48-1 respectively, after 48 weeks on the experiment. Dog on left, fed ad libitum, has more complete closure of epiphyseal growth plate, broader metaphysis, and a more obtuse angle between shaft and neck than in the case of the dog fed a restricted diet.

*Courtesy of Dr. Lennart Krook, New York
State College of Veterinary Medicine*

12½ pound pup is going to be normal, but it does point out an important idea: heavier pups have a significant *tendency* to become dysplastic and lighter pups, on the average, have more favorable odds of avoiding HD than the other group.

The Collie has a relatively low incidence of hip dysplasia, and is much slower growing in its first four months. Riser and Miller[71] report the weight of puppies to be half that of many other large breeds at the same age, which mature to approximately the same size. By the time the Collie is one and one-half years old, its weight approximates that of faster-maturing breeds of similar structure. It has not been as likely to deform the softer tissues of the hip joints during the slow change from cartilage to bone in the first six months or so of its life.

In comparisons with racing Greyhounds, researchers[28] found that German Shepherd Dogs, with a high incidence of hip dysplasia in the breed, have a higher growth rate and earlier skeletal maturation (size). Five-month old German Shepherd Dogs are con-

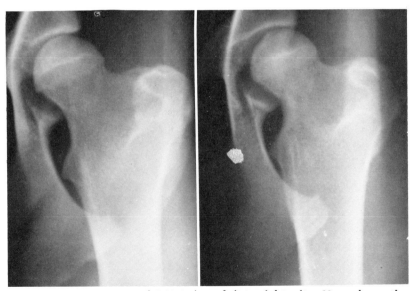

Fig. 10-12. Dogs A60-1 and R60-1, from left to right, after 60 weeks on the experiment. Again, the dog on the right, on a restricted but adequate diet, has a more normal (less obtuse) angle at which femoral head is inserted into the acetabulum and has a less thick neck than in the coxofemoral joint of its ad libitum partner.

Courtesy of Dr. Lennart Krook, New York
State College of Veterinary Medicine

sidered of equal skeletal "age" to six-month old Greyhounds.[41] Another report confirmed that slow growth was compatible with better hips[37,38] in comparison with rapidly growing individuals.

Bitches that must have their pups delivered by caesarean section ususally do not have early milk production, and often will take very little or no interest in caring for the pups. The first oral nutrient a normally-whelped pup gets is colostrum, and it was discovered[48] that colostrum-deprived, caesarean-delivered pups hand reared at consequently a greatly reduced rate of growth had a low incidence of hip dysplasia, while two "control" groups of naturally-whelped and bitch-fed pups grew at what was considered optimum or maximal rates, and had a high incidence of dysplasia.

An extremely important finding of the Cornell study, especially for the purchaser of a pup who wonders how much to feed it, is that even the dogs restricted to two-thirds the food consumption of the A-dogs had exceeded the caloric or metabolic requirements recommended in an authoritative text.[63] It was thought at first that the R-dogs were being somewhat deprived of an optimum intake, but it turned out that what was first thought of as restricted was really closer to optimum or even more, and the so-called optimum (ad libitum) diet was in actuality a case of over-nutrition. The dog owner who imagines he is barely fending off starvation in his hungry puppy with the pleading eyes and salivating mouth may even yet be overfeeding!

In short, the experiment indicated that feeding methods can affect production of growth hormones and the development of good bones and joints. Feeding must be restricted enough to keep growth rates sensible and less harmful, and a diet rich in calcium (even in proper ratio to phosphorus) is detrimental. Supplementation with calcium and Vitamin D is definitely contraindicated for growing puppies. So is overeating or a relatively high caloric intake. And the effects are largely irreversible; clinical signs of the disorders produced may never disappear.

Personal experience brings me to theorize that, as in the case of hip dysplasia, such osteochondritic disorders of the hip and other joints can be tremendously influenced by environmental forces such as overnutrition *in a dog genetically predisposed* to the disease or diseases. It may be that such problems as just described do not appear unless such genetic predisposition exists. One of our recent litters was whelped by a bitch that had previously produced some OFA-normal dogs as well as a couple dysplastic ones. This time, bred to an OFA-normal stud with good hip-pedigree-depth, she gave us four pups, all of which palpated a probable normal at eleven weeks, and X-rayed normal in the wedge view when nearly full-grown. The pups had ravenous appetites thanks to the competition at feeding time, grew rapidly, and always looked overweight. They had far-reaching gait, jumped high straight up from a standstill, chased each other and our Whippet all over the one-acre corral, and delighted in taking walks through the woods with me, where they could jump off boulders and run up the mountain. I did not check this litter for joint problems other than hip dysplasia, because there were no clinical signs telling me I should. But the genetic and phenotypic evidence was favorable in regard to hip dysplasia, so I continued to let this litter eat ad libitum, and experienced none of the problems of the test group of Great Danes in the 1974 Cornell study. All of these puppies recived OFA certification after two years of age.

The 1975 Stockholm Study

Another investigation in recent years[39] compared a group of dogs fed a relatively high caloric diet based on recommendations by the U.S. National Research Council (NRC),[56] which was paired with a group fed half as much, with calcium/phosphorus levels equalized between the two groups, until late in the program when they were given more to eat. The design of the experiment was carried out through five litters. Each member of a group was paired with a member of the other nutritional group on the basis of hip palpation results (both the Ortolani technique as modified by Mansson and Norberg,[64] and the Bardens technique),[3,4] weight, and sex. We'll look at just a couple of examples and then summarize.

Litter A consisted of eight German Shepherd Dog pups whose parents were dysplastic. They were divided into two groups: H (high) was fed the NRC diet, and L (low) got 50 percent of that amount. Because they were reared in a cold winter which increased their metabolism, their diets proved to be insufficient most of the time to produce any weight increase in group L and very little in group H, so increases over NRC levels were made a few times. The weights of all the L dogs stayed considerably under the standard growth curve for the breed, and only a couple H dogs reached it. Despite poor prognosis based on palpation at

ten weeks of age (laxity varied from 3 to 10 mm) *none* of litter A
was considered radiographically dysplastic at the age of 37 weeks
though no follow-up was done on the offspring of those dogs to
observe whether they were "genetically dysplastic," that is, if they
carried the genes for HD even though it did not show on X-ray
film at that young age (dogs are eligible for Swedish hip joint cer-
tificates as early as nine months old).

In litter B, eight Golden Retrievers were palpated, with 4 to
6 mm laxity. Both parents were dysplastic. Group H had a greater
than standard growth or weight gain, and group L was well below
the curve. All dogs in litter B were dysplastic except one "normal"
dog from group L at 34 weeks of age.

The sire of litter C had normal hips, at least by current Swedish standards, but he and the dysplastic dam of litter C had a common sire which had produced a high percentage of dysplasia. One
of the offspring, a group L dog, was declared normal at 43 weeks
(10 months); the rest were dysplastic.

The remaining litters in the program all were equally predisposed to HD, and like the others proved the influence of caloric
intake: "underfed" dogs in L groups had better hip configuration
than those fed twice as much, although none of them had any
signs of protein deficiency. Group H dogs also had greater severity
in the individual grades than had those in the L groups. Very few
dogs in all the litters had what were considered normal hips. It
must be noted that certification of normal, based on a standard
view radiograph, is not withheld until age two in Sweden as it is in
the United States. If it were, perhaps none at all would have radiographed normal.

But the key conclusions of the 1975 Stockholm work are that
hip dysplasia is more of a problem in dogs growing at a maximal
rate, that maximal growth is not as compatible with optimal skeletal development as is restricted feeding, and excessive weight gain,
even though it may appear standard to the owner, is well correlated with hip dysplasia *if the dog has a genetic trait for dysplasia.*
As Riser says,[70] "A variety of nutritional and mineral supplements
have been used in attempts to alter or prevent the course of hip
dysplasia in the dog. Diet has not affected the occurrence or
course of the disease other than the mechanical effect of
increased or decreased weight upon the hip joint."

SECTION IV
Control
Through Breeding

Chapter 11
Introduction
to Genetics

Hip dysplasia is not common in wild animals because of the continuing process of natural selection, i.e., only the fittest survive. In an environment where society removes or inhibits these means of selection, the host of ills of which hip dysplasia is but one example is denied full effect and allows the least fit to survive as well, and in some instances makes it easier. The hunter bags the biggest game, we cut the best trees down, and so forth.

The hypothetical young elk with hip dysplasia will be one of the first ones caught by the wolf pack, and its older companion in the herd, if its hips break down with arthritis before they should, will likewise end up as a meal before it can impregnate as many elk cows as the average male with normal hips can during its life-time. Conversely, the wolf with any dysplasia is not going to have the stamina of its normal packmates and, bothered by arthritis and coxo-femoral pain, is probably going to lose any challenge to its leadership as well as the concurrent privilege of fatherhood to a younger, more agile, normal-hipped male. In human society and in those animal societies we influence, these natural safeguards are often lost. In the wild, there are no welfare systems or hospitals.

A colony of Dingos (wild dog breed in Australia) has been reported[2,44] which has been bred, fed, reared, and protected in captivity for some 40 years. When radiographed, a substantial portion of these zoo animals were found to be dysplastic. Conversely, newly captured Dingos were free of the disorder.

"Canine hip dysplasia, a multifactorial, developmental, quantitative condition, is genetically controlled."[39] Early in the 1960's and before, hip dysplasia was considered to be due to one or more dominant genes with incomplete penetrance,[37,59,76] which meant it varied from individual to individual, or even between one hip and the other in the same dog. It is now more widely held that hip dysplasia is basically a recessive trait (and recessive here does not mean bashful or unnoticed). To understand the difference, and to gain a working knowledge of the inheritability of hip dysplasia, with an eye toward genetically controlling it in one's kennel or breed, a brief biology lesson and a simplified example of inheritance mode would be helpful.

In every cell of every living thing, there are submicroscopic strands of protein-like material called "chromosomes," composed of long, spiral macromolecules.* An electron microscope can differentiate not only the number but also the shapes and sizes of chromosomes when cells divide. The dog has 78 chromosomes, humans normally have 46; always an even number since chromosomes appear in pairs, with each cell containing the same number of chromosomes except in sex cells which each have half the number. The male sperm and the female ovum (egg cell) each have one of each pair found in the other cells of the body.

A chromosome is composed of innumerable chemical units called "genes," from which we get the word *genetics*. The structure and nature of genes have, until the present date, been known not so much by visual observation (at 1,000 times magnification separate genes are still indistinct) as by deductive reasoning, much the same way the planet Pluto and moons of other planets have been predicted long before technology made them "visible." (Early in 1979 a newspaper article claimed that even individual genes were "visible" with a new technique.) An idea of how complex genetics can be is had when one realizes there may be from 10,000 to 100,000 pairs of genes in mammals. The interaction of many of these genes makes for an almost infinite number of variations, like snowflakes or fingerprints, and no two dogs are exactly alike. Genetic diseases such as hip dysplasia are results of one or more abnormalities in deoxyribonucleic acid (DNA), the complex chemical of which genes are primarily made.

Remember that genes operate in pairs, as do chromosomes. When the chromosomes and genes of sex cells are united at conception, the physical characteristics dictated by one gene may be different than the characteristic of its corresponding gene-partner, in which case the animal is said to be heterozygous for the trait exhibited. If the chemical nature (molecular structure) of the two members of that pair of genes is identical, the animal is homozy-

---

*Macro-: large; Molecules are fairly stable combinations of atoms. Examples of macromolecules include: cellulose, DNA, nylon, rubber.

gous for the trait in question. The prefix homo- means "the same," and hetero- means "different." "Zygo-" is Greek for "pair." Different traits are determined by different genes located at specific places (singular: locus, plural: loci) on the chromosome. Most traits are a result of several genes interacting, with more than one locus involved, as in the colors of blue Doberman Pinschers, liver-and-tan German Shepherd Dogs, Weimeraners, etc. or even more complicated expressions.

In a heterozygous situation, one gene will have a greater influence than its partner. This is why a dog will favor one parent in certain characteristics rather than the other parent. When a trait is determined by a single pair of genes, it is referred to as a "simple Mendellian trait." An example: among the coat colors acceptable for Labrador Retrievers are solid black and solid yellow. A homozygous black bred to a homozygous yellow will produce heterozygous black pups; each pup will inherit one gene for black from one parent and one gene for yellow from the other parent. The gene for black is expressed in the pups' coat color in preference to the gene for yellow, hence all pups are black in color (phenotype). But because they each have a yellow gene in the pair on the coat-color locus, they are said to carry the "recessive" for yellow, and the trait is expressed in a simple, obvious, complete way: black coats. Many diseases and traits are passed on to progeny in this manner, but more are complicated in comparison. The pups mentioned, by the way, can produce yellow offspring as a result of being carriers of that allele (an allele is one of a pair of genes).

Most inherited characteristics are not simple, and are results of several genes interacting. Examples of complex inherited traits are temperament, hunting ability, belligerence, gunshyness, methods of playing, length of bone, and hip dysplasia. Such inheritance is described as being polygenic (many genes). As mentioned earlier, polygenic defects are especially subject to influence in their expression by the myriad forces of environment. Some disorders appear to be 50 to 100 percent genetic in expression, and others primarily due to environmental factors. Or it could be phrased that genetically determined diseases are modified to a degree somewhere between zero and 99+ percent by forces other than the genes themselves.

It was stated that hip dysplasia is generally accepted today as being not only polygenic, but recessive in nature. Just as a breeder can reach a point where all his Labs are yellow (a recessive color) or his German Shepherd Dogs mostly black-and-tan (recessive to sable pattern), one can reach a point where most of the dogs in a given breed or colony are dysplastic. Dominance does not guarantee prevalence.

Patterson[62] illustrates polygenic inheritance with a balance: one pan contains the "good hip genes," the other contains the "bad hip genes." Each gene is on a different locus, and the pans probably involve more than one chromosome. Each pair of genes has one partner (allele) from the sire and one allele from the dam. Suppose there were 50 pairs (100 genes) having some influence on hip dysplasia (an arbitrary, perhaps wild, guess). If young Rover had radiographically fair hips (rated normal), and 48 of his hip genes were defective, the other 52 okay, and if he is bred to Lady who also has "normal X-rays," and 48 of *her* genes are likewise defective, what will the puppies of such a union inherit?

Mathematically, one might expect more possibilities than the dam could ever produce, but suppose one of her pups designated "A" inherits 24 of Rover's bad genes and 24 of Lady's bad genes (which means it received 26 good genes from each parent). "A" will then have the same genetic bank: 48 bad, 52 good. Littermate "B" could easily have 75 percent bad, 25 percent good genes, and its hips may be more likely to look bad on radiographs than A's, other things being equal. Littermate "C" might inherit 50 good genes from each, and since 50 is the maximum available from each parent, zero bad genes. Highly unlikely. Let's forget about the B and C types now for the following illustration:

Let us further suppose Rover and Lady are bred to each other by a university mathematics instructor (named Matthew Maddox, of course) and the "average" pup in his litter has 48 bad, 52 good genes. Professor Maddox kept one of the average pups, "Gordo," and fed it a diet laced with calcium/phosphorus/Viatmin D tablets, and beefed up that diet with ground meat (pun intentional) to insure a hearty appetite, but kept the additive meat to 10 percent or less of each meal, corresponding to the advice of his colleague, the biology professor who used to work for NRC. Another average pup, "Slim," was sold very early to a student who spends his summers at the Royal Veterinary College in Stockholm, helping researchers compile data on the effects of overnutrition. Knowing what you do about the influence of diet, especially overnutrition,[30] guess which of these two average pups will have the greater chance of clinical and radiographic hip dysplasia.

One more supposition is that the rest of Lady's large litter (all average) went to loving homes whose masters all made sure they had their shots and vitamins, and ate well of their nice, rich puppy food especially formulated for growing dogs, and reeking with appetizing flavors.

By now, you're getting way ahead of me. Professor Matthew Maddox who spent a lot of money for a brood bitch and a stud service, with perhaps both animals having OFA numbers, has turned out a large litter of pups which have become badly dysplastic before the one-year guarantee ran out, and has to borrow money to make refunds to some of the unlucky buyers, and stave off the others with a promise of a free replacement as soon as he can get another litter out of Lady, sired by some stud other than that rascal, Rover! Maybe when that student gets back from Sweden this fall, just in time to breed Slim when Lady comes into season? What luck!: the only dog not sold to a show home has great hips . . . well, actually, the OFA said "fair," but at least he's not dysplastic, and breeding to retain Lady's good features as well as Slim's would be great! Besides, Lady's breeders had told him they didn't have dysplasia in their kennel, so it *must* have been carried by Rover. Maybe he could talk that student into a free stud service or a pup in exchange. But you and I know something the professor doesn't: Slim has exactly the same hip genotype or genetic bank as his sire Rover, and all of Slim's littermates. And with such a precarious balance, such a small margin of good genes over bad, the influence of environment will again be tremendous.

Unfortunately, "breeding programs" similar to the above extreme example are being conducted in like manner by "breeders" all over the world. The cripples go to the pound, or are nursed by longsuffering, disappointed, or embittered owners, and the others, like Slim and even some with not as good radiographs or none taken at all, are bred and bred and bred. There are thousands of dogs and cats born every hour,* 87.6 million (HSUS figure) each year![22, 34] We have a responsibility to encourage the breeding of genetically better dogs in preference to dogs with relatively more defective genes.

Perhaps someday something on the order of a blood test or retina examination may detect "carriers," or dogs which are phe-

---

*Dr. Faulkner[62] says 2,000 to 3,000; Humane Society of U.S. says 10,000; United Humanitarians say 12,500; Roger Caras estimates 15,000.

notypically normal (no clinical signs, good standard view radiograph, good thigh muscles), but heterozygous for hip dysplasia, carriers or possessors of too high a proportion of defective hip genes to be good for their breeds. Carriers of hemophilia or of red blood cell enzyme deficiency can be detected with blood tests today; maybe PRA, hip dysplasia, and heart disease carriers can be detected tomorrow.

The great battles in human medicine are now being fought in two fields: environment and research. The big people-killers today are cancer (cigarettes, air pollutants, and a multitude of natural and synthetic chemicals that add to our "cancer load"), cirrhosis (socially or environmentally-encouraged heavy drinking), heart and circulatory disorders (diet, lack of exercise), arthritis (perhaps weather), and similarly environmental diseases, as opposed to yesteryear's diseases of clearer etiology when specific disorders were found to be caused by specific bacilli, vitamin deficiencies, and viruses. But the president of the Sloan-Kettering Cancer Center believes[84] that even the diseases we here recognize as largely influenced by environment (polygenic?) will also be knocked off one by one with the advance of scientific research. At the center of each such disease, he says, is a switch waiting to be found and flipped, suddenly halting or turning that disease around in its tracks.

Perhaps it will turn out that schizophrenia is a neurochemical disorder with a single chemical event gone awry, that arthritis is caused by an as-yet-undiscovered single agent, and vascular problems such as stroke, high blood pressure, coronary occlusion, and cholesterol build-up are centrally caused by abnormal genes, magnified or amplified by adverse environments. And perhaps someday the mysterious, chemical nature of the inheritance of defects will be understood, and a simple chemical correction made. We can dream. Until then, we must use what tools we have and do what can be done to control the genetic disorder known as hip dysplasia.

Chapter 12
Some
Recommendations

Patterson[62] is optimistic about the prospect of great strides in knowledge of genetic diseases of both man and other animals, and predicts that concerned dog breeders will continue to see many improvements in diagnosis, treatment, and control of genetic disorders. It is this group of concerned breeders, as well as their customers and veterinarians, that we are attempting to encourage with this book.

What can be done about controlling genetic diseases? Whether in one's own kennel or on a larger scale, four ingredients besides time are recommended:

1. Information. What is the mode of inheritance?

2. Accurate diagnosis. Is the standard radiograph enough?

3. Identification of carriers. Blood tests in the future? Progeny tests (after breeding)? Wedge radiographs (before breeding?

4. A real breeding program. Breed only non-carriers or those with the best genetic bank for good hips.

If the aim of the breeder reading this book is to eliminate or significantly reduce the incidence of hip dysplasia in his own breeding program, then he should do all possible to reduce, in successive generations, the proportion of bad hip genes in his stock. The preponderance of alleles must be non-defective; the balance pan of good genes must be as full as possible. Specifically, how does one work toward that goal?

Education

Expanding further on the four-step fight against genetic diseases, the more accurate information one has, the faster the results. Sometimes there are plateaus to overcome. Like breaking the sound barrier or turning on a light switch, a shade more effort or a little more knowledge can mean the difference in a sudden and significant improvement.

Before Mendel, environment was believed the prime or sole shaper of life to the extent that even those who considered themselves searchers for truth and possessors of knowledge believed in such things as spontaneous generation, and that babies would reflect or look like whatever frightened their mothers during pregnancy. Today we know that mice are not formed from straw and rags, and that dogs don't get mean simply from eating raw meat. After acceptance of the "scientific method" and the discovery of genetics, the pendulum swung sharply in the new direction. A plateau had been reached and new horizons were suddenly brought into focus.

In the late 1950's and early 60's it was thought that heritability of hip dysplasia was around 0.6 (60 percent) but experiments in Sweden and elsewhere gave the present heritability index value of 0.2 to 0.3, a medium heritability for a quantitative trait. Thus, 0.25 would mean that 25 percent of the phenotypic variance is due to gene action. This does not mean, however, that 75 percent of the dysplasia in dogs is *caused* by environment. The cause lies in the genes, but the incidence and severity are to some degree determined by external factors. One of those plateaus just over the next ridge might be the discovery that dogs such as the racing Greyhound and colonies of other breeds with practically zero defective hip genes might be unaffected in that joint by the overnutrition discussed in a previous chapter and elsewhere.[30,45]

Diagnosis

The second ingredient would be an adequate means of spotting the dysplastic or predysplastic dog. The wedge radiograph has already been described; its proponents point to the fact that all newly-born pups are as normal as can be determined radiographically, and that different individuals will show abnormal remodelling and laxity at different ages, some few not until 36 months of age, and a fraction of a percent perhaps not until halfway through life. Since joint laxity is, if not a prime cause, at least a related feature in hip dysplasia, the ability to demonstrate it early in a dog which radiographs normal in the standard view is a valuable addition to diagnosis. A key word is "early," since there is not very much difference in the percentages reported detected between standard and wedge views over the age of two years: Bardens claims the wedge will increase the detection of hip dysplasia by 10 percent at age two years, but by as much as 30 percent at age one year.[7] The wedge should be viewed as merely another breeders' tool, not the only tool, and not the final answer. But neither should any tool be neglected because that one tool cannot give all the answers.

Prediagnostic Identification: Palpation

The two most widely used prediagnostic techniques for determining carriers of hip dysplasia in the *young* dog are the wedge radiograph and the Bardens method of palpating puppies. The term prediagnostic is used because at a young age a diagnosis of hip dysplasia based on the accepted definitions and radiological and other descriptions cannot be made with certainty. In most cases hip dysplasia cannot be visually proven at the ages pups are generally palpated: eight to twelve weeks; it is a prediction, as weather forecasts are predictions, based on a pattern of events or signs which have preceded something with some degree of reliability and repetitiveness. This prediction is based partly on the theory[4] that the pup with a genetically defective mechanism for hip formation develops not only joint laxity, but a pectineus spasm as well. The muscle in contracture levers the femoral head out of the acetabulum. Faster growth of the femur in certain breeds and individuals exerts greater such forces before the rim of the acetabulum ossifies. One can throw out the myopathy part of the theory with no damage at all to the prediagnostic value of puppy palpation.

The Bardens technique can be learned by the veterinarian reading the instructions in the Proceedings of the 1972 OFA Symposium[4,6] (available from OFA with a donation suggested by this author) but not nearly as well as being shown, in person, by an experienced palpator, much as learning to paint or play the violin. Accuracy increases with proper technique and a feel for the art. It likewise is not the final, total answer to hip dysplasia, nor the single quickest route to its elimination, but its proponents claim greater accuracy than the standard radiograph taken at approximately one year of age. The claim is that even using a lopsided comparison, the 30 percent error factor in radiographing one-year-old dogs is greater than the 15 to 20 percent error factor in palpating eight-week-old pups, and that as one looks at standard radiographs at younger ages vs. palpation at older ages, the value or advantage of palpation is obvious. Regardless of percentages, the value of another tool for the breeder should be appreciated.

Palpation should not be used in place of radiographs, but in conjunction with them in building a breeding program to get rid of dysplasia. The major benefit is that the breeder can cull his litter early and, if necessary, dispose of the worst before some buyer is faced with the costs of subsequent veterinary care including medication, surgery, and possible euthanasia of a dysplastic dog.[24] Worse than the economic problem or the damage to the breeder's reputation is the psychological effect on the buyer of a cute, cuddly puppy which grows up to be abnormal and in pain. The cost of palpating a litter is peanuts compared to the costs in rearing the dysplastic dogs to adulthood, then selling them at a loss because of lower marketability and having to make good on some sales later on.

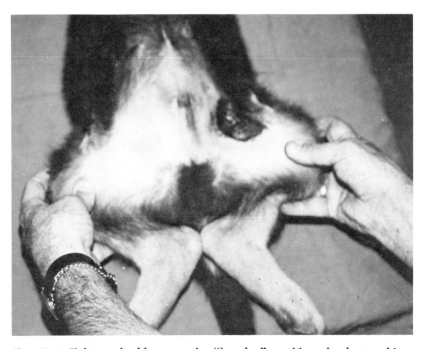

Fig. 12-1. Eight-week-old puppy in "frog-leg" position, hocks touching. Note spot of black ink in preparation for tattoo identification.

Courtesy of Dr. R. W. Huff

Prior to adopting the practice of palpation, the Eye Dog Foundation, a guide dog school in California, had a 55 percent incidence of hip dysplasia in the puppies they produced as candidates for guide dogs. After their veterinarian was trained in the technique mentioned above, and after they also implemented wedge radiography in addition to puppy palpation, the incidence dropped to 15 percent in 2½ years[4] and in four years it was down to 5 percent.[7] The "Eye Dog Foundation Science Award" dated October 23, 1970, and signed by its director at that time, Erich Renner* states, "Because of his work, many more dogs can now serve the blind." All puppies were palpated at eight weeks and again at six months, then the ones passing both times were reared by 4-H children and their families until one year or older at which

*Mr. Renner is now Training Director for International Guiding Eyes, Inc. of North Hollywood, Calif.

**This award was presented to Dr. John W. Bardens, who developed the most commonly used palpation technique.

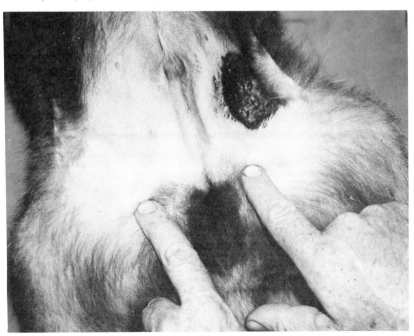

Fig. 12-2. Pectineus muscle being palpated. If muscle (at fingertips) is abnormally taut, it will be prominent as shown here.

Courtesy of Dr. R. W. Huff

time they returned to the school for standard and wedge radiographs. Those with a normal reading in all three methods were trained for guide work and made eligible for breeding.

The Foundation's dogs had been described as having hips like Greyhounds, but were without a doubt attractive representatives of their breed (most guide dogs are German Shepherd Dogs). Some of the males were as heavy as 120 pounds, which is 40 pounds greater than the breed standard recommends, and one would ordinarily connect oversize with a higher incidence of hip dysplasia were it not for the genetic selection and the prediagnostic screening used here. The dogs have been described as big-boned, massive, with good angulation, good muscle development, excellent temperament, and of sufficient "type" to look respectable in the show ring. The influence of the environment in that col-

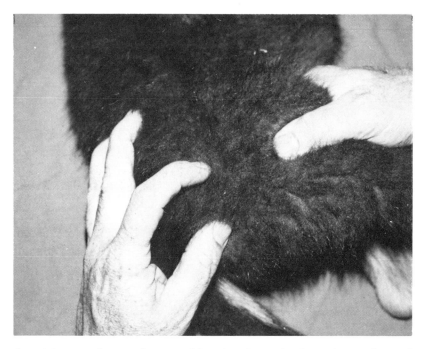

Fig. 12-3. Lateral recumbent position for determination of coxo-femoral joint laxity. Index finger of left hand is on joint; right hand lifts femur.

Courtesy of Dr. R. W. Huff

ony has been decreased through selective breeding for dogs whose hips are relatively unaffected by the external factors. [49]

Identifying the carriers of hip dysplasia (the genotypically dysplastic yet phenotypically normal dogs) may be a matter of adhering to a strict control program such as that used by the Eye Dog Foundation in the early 70's: utilizing a combination of palpation and wedge radiography. The great advantage over progeny testing, which will be discussed further in the next chapter, can be understood when one sees the pet population figures as estimated by the Humane Society of the U.S. It can be done before, or instead of, breeding rather than after breeding.

Step number four in Patterson's recipe involves so much background and discussion that it will be covered in a separate chapter, the one immediately following.

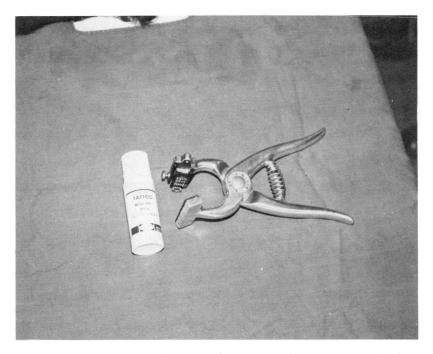

Fig. 12-4. Tattoo clamp and ink for identification of pup at time of palpation. (Electric pen may be used instead of clamp.)

Courtesy of Dr. R. W. Huff

Chapter 13
Breeding
Programs

The fourth ingredient in controlling this polygenic disease, hip dysplasia, is to breed only the non-carriers or those with the best genetic bank for good hips: a good breeding program, in other words.

Let's look at some earlier attempts to find what was hoped would be such a good program. The hereditary basis of the disease is well recognized, but regardless of the factors which in recent years have been found to precipitate or increase the severity of hip dysplasia, "its etiology and pathogenesis have not yet been defined."[50] This is only part of the reason progress has been spotty and relatively slow, another major facet being the failure of most breeders to stick with a really rigorous program of control.

Hutt has written[35] regarding environmental influences, such as restricted nutrition which can mask hip dysplasia, that "they will be used for that purpose . . . most breeders will do their utmost to provide the environment that will cause the least dysplasia. Genes which induce that defect will thus be masked and therefore retained in the stock. Few breeders are likely to provide knowingly the adverse environment that would reveal such genes." While good judgment is still required when feeding and breeding mentally and physically sound dogs,[40] a structurally and genetically sound hip is likely to stay structurally sound.

The Fidelco Experiment

A number of breeding programs have been reported in the literature.[7,32,37,53] Kaman and Gossling reduced the incidence of hip dysplasia, as radiographically observable in ten-month or older dogs, in a program designed to reduce the rejection rate of dogs intended for use as guide dogs for the blind. The Fidelco Breeders Foundation had been selecting mainly on the basis of temperament and trainability, using leading German bloodlines as the foundation stock and including many prominent American and German dog show winners in the pedigrees. However, it was soon discovered that most of the animals they produced were dysplastic to some degree, and that this was the case with the foundation stock as well. It wasn't that only show dogs carried the problem. The majority of German Shepherd Dogs were affected. Normal and near-normal dogs had to be found.

A gradual beginning was probably necessary because at the start normal dogs were so hard to come by, as the Foundation was limited in knowledge, dog donations, and funds. As more dogs became available it was possible to increase selection. Even using partners free of dysplasia by the above lenient measure, an unacceptable incidence remained in the offspring. Better results were obtained when a greater number of the ancestors had good hips, and when pedigree depth was considered in the choices of brood bitches and studs. Partway through the program a disappointing lack of progress forced Fidelco to select dogs from original sheep-herding strains, since nature, through the rigorous lifestyle of the shepherds' dogs, had already selected for sound movement and stamina over many generations. Von Stephanitz, the founder of the German Shepherd Dog breed, tells[87] of a nine-year old dog entered in the champion stakes for sheepwork in 1919, which had to run for three hours in the sun behind his owner's bicycle to reach the contest, then took part in the competition, and again ran three hours home, in order to start work with the flocks! The average sheep dog at the time was running 20 miles a day during working hours. More demands are made on the hips of such a dog than on most wild animals, and this is the type of dog shepherds would breed their bitches to, the type Fidelco hoped would solve their selection problems. In order to simulate a little of such selection in show dogs, many dogs in Germany had to pass agility and endurance tests leading to Schutzhund and AD* degrees. In 1960, Dr. Funck, then president of the SV, said that HD was not a problem if the dog could trot for 25 miles and finish that exercise with no signs of lameness.[11] The reason racing Greyhounds are free of dysplasia is that the ones which fail to run a certain distance in a certain time are destroyed and do not contribute to the breed's population, or "gene pool."

---

*AD is a training degree awarded in Germany, denoting successful completion of endurance testing routines.

Improvement in Fidelco's program was noticed immediately with the introduction of these strains. At the time, OFA was but an idea forming in the minds of a few, and radiographic data on older or deceased German dogs were just not available. What Fidelco and its breeders looked for, then, was information regarding sound movement and strength in old age as criteria for pedigree choice, as well as the phenotype of the dogs being secured, and of their parents. One of the contributing factors in improvement may have been the practice of outcrossing, although in essence it may have had only an indirect bearing. The Germans have historically been reluctant to use much close linebreeding or inbreeding, and the pedigrees of the sheepherding strains reflected that. The work of Scott and Fuller at Bar Harbor, Maine[38] concluded in part that linebreeding often "spread unknown and unseen recessives," and since Fidelco had such poor luck with linebred American show stock, they erroneously attributed their problem partly to that breeding practice, and implemented outcrossing and the use of sheepherding strains at the same time. If linebred dogs with the same genetic banks had been available, they would have served as well. Additional Fidelco guidelines included pelvic muscle mass, growth rate, adult size and weight, and skeletal structure such as croup angle and rear limb angulation.

The Bar Harbor and Fidelco assumptions gave the impression that linebreeding per se is contrary to good practice regarding elimination of hip dysplasia and, by inference, other characteristics as well. Actually, outcrossing is more likely to mask the bad recessive genes and pass them on, hidden from notice, to successive generations. One case in point: a well-known Michigan breeder with many select and R.O.M. dogs* in his kennel has consistently used intensive linebreeding and inbreeding on a relatively few ancestors, and his dogs in general have an admirable reputation for normal hips. Linebreeding on good hips can only improve the breed, while outcrossing can hide bad hip genes for generations, if those bred had a significant proportion of bad genes.

---

*"Select" refers to roughly the top 10 percent of the champions at the national specialty show, and "R.O.M." (Register of Merit) is a title based on the ability to produce champions. These are used in a breed in which it is notoriously difficult to win championships.

BREEDING TERMS

Bloodlines   Ancestral tracing of the "family tree" in regard to certain individuals in the pedigree. Inherited factors were once thought to be carried and transmitted by the blood. Today the word is used out of habit and convenience; "genetic lines" would be more accurate.

Inbreeding   Mating of very close relatives: father/daughter, grandmother/grandson, brother/sister, etc. There is no fine semantic line between inbreeding and linebreeding, only a relative matter of degree.

Linebreeding Mating of animals which share some common ancestor(s), thus presumably increasing the likelihood of inheriting that ancestor's desirable phenotype. The sharing generally occurs in the first four or five generations, ignoring those further back. Extend pedigrees far enough, and you'll find all individuals in a breed have some common ancestors on both sides back to the origin of the breed.

Outcrossing The opposite of linebreeding. The fewer ancestors shared by both parents, and the further back, the more the dog is outcrossed. You can breed two heavily linebred dogs to each other and have an outcross if the same ancestor doesn't appear early in both sire's and dam's sides of the pedigree.

Phenotype   Outward appearance. Unless you know something of the near ancestors, siblings, and progeny of a dog, its phenotype may give you very little to base your breeding on. Radiographs show part of the phenotype.

Genotype   The actual genetic make-up of a dog, some characteristics being obvious in the phenotype, some partially masked (as in a few simple recessive traits), and some completely hidden (as in many polygenic recessives).

Abbreviations "Bernd 4, 5, 6—3,5; Lance 3—3" means that Bernd appears three times in the sire's pedigree (in the pup's fourth, fifth, and sixth generations) and twice in the dam's pedigree (in the pup's third and fifth generations. This pup's sire was linebred on a Bernd grandson (Mike 2—3), but since the dam had no Mike in her line, the pup is not linebred on Mike at all.

Some European Breeding Programs

The Swedish Kennel Club, in cooperation with the Royal Veterinary College, bred and recorded more than 11,000 German Shepherd Dogs over a ten-year period and ended the decade in 1969 with as much dysplasia and as many severe cases as when they began, while in Switzerland it was shown that a strictly controlled program using "only animals with radiographically normal or near-normal hip joints"[58] could lower incidence to 20 percent in a few years. A similar program among Swedish breeders of Golden Retrievers and Labrador Retrievers led to considerable improvement. Why the difference?

One factor may be the young age at which Sweden has certified dogs as normal (9 months and up), while such dogs are very possibly genetically unsound and may even develop clinical and radiological signs after maturing and breeding and passing the defect on to its progeny. Probably a greater factor is the lack of adherence to what Lust calls "a protocol of selection which is . . . capable of ensuring systematic genetic progress."[49]

Breeders in Sweden were probably giving more emphasis to desired "fad" characteristics such as extreme rear angulation or the impression of great "reach" in front, or a sloping topline, rather than to good hips and a strict interpretation of the breed standard which was originally written to describe a sound, functional dog. This has also been quite true in the United States and has undoubtedly decelerated progress in the control of hip dysplasia. Some U.S. breeders have gotten on the right track, only to be wooed away by a flashy, good-looking champion, even though said champion may not have been radiographically or genetically free of hip dysplasia. Use of such a stud may mean two steps backwards in one's breeding program.

The Swedes likewise have held in low esteem the importance of selection against hip dysplasia; among the ten most used sires in 1971, one which was not radiographed produced *at least* 56 percent dysplastic offspring (remember the age possible for definition of normal). Seventy-two percent of his get were born by dysplastic and non-radiographed bitches. Apparently the American tradition of collecting a stud fee for service to any live bitch shipped in (whether she can stand or has to be propped up, muzzled, and tranquilized) is mirrored in some other countries. Audell[58] reports another normal stud, bred to bitches, 68 percent of whom were normal, produced 57 percent dysplasia in his offspring. It was noted that many of the sires used in Sweden, as is the case to a lesser extent in many breeds in the United States, were German imports, about whose parents' and grandparents' hips little is known. Apathy and vacillation admit to no national boundaries.

Selection on the Basis of Pelvic Muscle Mass

It has been observed[71] that a high muscle mass ratio is correlated with a low incidence of hip dysplasia. To demonstrate that pelvic muscle mass is an inherited rather than a conditioned characteristic, a comparison of different breeds was made (see the last sub-heading in Chapter 6). Normal-hipped dogs had a higher average muscle mass index than dysplastic dogs.

Only in the case of Sighthounds would speed tests have any meaning, and then not much, since a great deal of winning is determined as much if not more by desire on the part of the coursing hound, as by hip status. In the case of many other breeds and individuals, the ability or eagerness to run a fixed distance in a limited time (which is the life/death criterion[44] in selecting track Greyhounds) is far removed from the quality of the hip joints. "In the selection of . . . German Shepherds and July Foxhounds, there has been less and sometimes no regard for the musculature, speed, or hindquarter power."[70,74] Perhaps the most sensible use of an estimation of the pelvic muscle mass index of a prospective puppy purchase or choice of a breeding animal might be to examine the dog's hindquarters by sight and feel, then make a subjective evaluation. One could add that information, in its proper perspective, to all the other data available on the dog, radiographic and palpation data perhaps being at the head of the list, along with radiographic data on near ancestors and siblings. It would be unwieldy to measure with calipers the thickness of the thigh, compute that against the weight of the dog, then compare with other pups or dogs of identical weight and after the same number of hours following evacuation of stomach and intestinal contents. How much easier and surer to rely on the more objective means such as radiography. However, if other data appear satisfactory, and the thighs appear to indicate a low pelvic mass compared to other individuals, one might be wise to recheck the former data.

Progeny Testing

Progeny testing has been attempted and recommended several times. Simply stated, it involves a measure of a dog's genotype or relative number of good hip genes arrived at by comparing the phenotypes (radiographs, especially) of its offspring with those of other dogs. One of the studs used by Sweden's Armed Forces Dog Training Center, diagnosed as having excellent hips at five years of age, produced a frequency of 28 percent dysplasia out of five brood bitches. Another stud, with excellent hips at nine years of age, produced 60 percent dysplasia when bred to the same five bitches.[32] Progeny testing concludes that the former stud dog is preferable to the latter in a program to reduce the incidence of hip dysplasia.

A serious disadvantage to progeny testing as a means of control has been illustrated in a previous chapter. First, the answers are available only after a considerable number of puppies have been added to the pet population problem, a near-crisis in some areas. Secondly, claims are likely to be vague and misleading. A popular national specialty winner may be used so often that he produces hundreds of OFA-certified dogs, yet has a "success rate" of only 25 percent, while another champion placing further down on the totals of Best Of Breeds won, used on fewer bitches, and consequently producing fewer pups, may have a success rate of 75 percent. The owner of stud dog number 1 isn't going to broadcast the enormous number of dysplastic pups, yet will point gladly to dozens of OFA-normal progeny winning in the ring. If *all* progeny could be evaluated, and an accurate statistic published on "percent normals produced," progeny testing could be a valid approach within a breed. But the AKC is not set up to withhold registrations until hips are certified, and neither U.S. breed clubs nor the OFA have authority to do so, thus progeny testing is only good on a limited scale such as in individual breeding kennels.

An ad hoc committee appointed by the Scandinavian Kennel Clubs has submitted specific recommendations on progeny testing:[58] The proposed sire first must be radiographed normal at a minimum age of one year and pass a given mental (temperament) test. He is then bred to at least three bitches, which are offspring of at least three different sires. The bitches must also pass the radiograph and mental tests, and 35 of their collective offspring should be registered and tattooed. At least 80 percent must be radiographed after reaching one year, and take the mental test. The sire would be declared suitable for further breeding if he produces a combination of 75 percent normals and 60 percent mentally sound pups. A lesser quantity in good hip production could be tolerated if the mental soundness ratio were high; examples: 70 percent hips/75 percent "heads," or 65 percent hips/90 percent heads.

Selective Rating Systems

In 1972 a scheme was proposed[18] to the Canadian Kennel Club (not adopted) in which an official notation would be made on the registration documents, somewhat along the lines of the SV "a" stamp on German pedigrees. Four categories were suggested, each progressively more desirable from a breeding standpoint:

1. Normal radiograph

2. The individual plus its sire and dam are normal

3. The individual plus four full siblings are normal

4. The individual and most of its progeny are normal.

I would like to suggest that in America it may be possible to establish through the OFA a similar rating system:

1. Existing (1981) OFA requirements met for normal, including "fair."

2. A one-star rating: normal two-year or older radiograph graded good or excellent in either the standard view or with a wedge.

3. A two-star rating: normal (good or excellent) radiograph, plus both parents rated normal as in the first category or better.

4. A three-star rating: meet the requirements for two stars plus: produce 70 percent one-star progeny when bred to a one-star partner, or produce 80 percent one-star progeny when bred to a partner with two stars, or produce 90 percent one-star progeny when bred to a three-star partner.

Percentages in the fourth category would be based on at least two breedings with two different partners which are not siblings to each other. The AKC need not even become involved. (It is reluctant to move from its responsibilities in pedigree registration and in shows and trials.) Participation would be encouraged by competitive pressure, consumer demand, and good "P.R." on the part of the OFA, veterinarians, breeders, breed clubs, and dog publications. Breeds relatively unaffected by hip dysplasia would lose no status, nor would OFA-certified dogs whose owners are recalcitrant or satisfied with their certifications. The star rating would be a goal to reach toward for those who desire something extra either as a status symbol (that's what the OFA number is to many) or as a means of eliminating hip dysplasia as a problem. It would be no burden on those who did not wish to participate and compete, if they were able to sell all they produced satisfactorily without the added ratings.

The Bardens Breeding Program

The control program recommended by Bardens,[7] and one which is represented by several colonies of dogs now producing 99-100 percent normals, begins with an admission demanded of the breeder that he acknowledges hip dysplasia in his kennel, perhaps even some of his best dogs are dysplastic, and that he wants to eliminate hip dysplasia from his kennel. Wedge radiographs are taken and palpations are performed on all young breeding prospects in an attempt to detect dysplasia carriers. A breeding-normal hip is distinguished from a functionally-normal hip with these two procedures used to determine or guess at which animals have the lowest genetic pool for dysplasia, or at least the best chance of having such. Thirdly, the breeder decides if there are any dysplastic dogs other than the Grade 3 or Grade 4 specimens, that should remain in the program to contribute certain other desirable qualities (ones that cannot be obtained from other normal dogs). If so, that dog (or dogs) is bred to those members of its progeny with the best hips or those progeny are bred to each other and a more demanding selection made from that ensuing generation.

Offspring are palpated between eight and twelve weeks, again at six months, and once more at a year of age at which time both a wedge radiograph and a standard-view radiograph are taken and compared. Laxity should be 0.5 mm or less on palpation and both radiographs should be able to meet OFA's standards for normal. If there are not enough offspring passing these tests, the best of the lot could be bred, delaying optimum results for a generation but perhaps retaining some other desired characteristics. However, the longer one waits to attain 100 percent or near it, the more likely he is to drop out of the program and be satisfied with partial results, only to encounter the problem again later.

After working with several breeders and breeds, the claim was made that one can expect 80 percent normal in the first generation of breeding normal to normal (as measured by the above method), 90 percent in the second generation (breeding back to a parent), and 100 percent by the fourth generation. It should be emphasized that these claims and figures are based on an evaluation of normal as seen in both radiographic views: standard and wedge. A dysplasia Grade 1 dog which is graded as such on the basis of palpation and wedge radiograph even though it may have normal hips in the standard view at the same age is said to produce about 40 percent wedge-normals in the first generation when bred to a wedge-normal partner. Also, most of the breeding prospects are screened at an early age, before the breeder puts a couple of years feed and care into them, and young enough to fit them into breeding plans. If all partners were bred only after they had attained an age of three years, when 97 percent or 98 percent of the dysplastic individuals can have been identified, results would probably be similar to those in the Bardens program.

The figures are a small portion of the statistics compiled over a period of 15 years and 18,000 pups palpated,[44] with an average of 400 radiographs of breeding stock per year as well as follow-up radiographs of dogs previously palpated as puppies.

An example of using a dysplastic dog in a successful breeding program is the story of "Champ." I have elected to use an alias for him even though the dog has been publicly identified and his story told elsewhere. Champ was twice National Amateur Champion, three times Canadian National Champion, twice National Senior Open Champion, and all-time high-point field trial dog in America. Champ was radiographed as Grade 1 in one hip. Bred to a palpated-normal, wedge-normal bitch, he produced 50 percent normals in what we'll call the X-litter. (When bred to a near-normal* bitch, Champ produced six dysplastic and two normal pups.) Bred to one of those normal "X" pups, he produced a 60 percent normal litter. One of Champ's normal X-litter pups was bred to a wedge-normal bitch and they produced two dysplastic pups and eight normal ones (80 percent normal rate). Of course, the fewer the examples, the less scientific the conclusions about statistics, but it is felt these results were typical.

Two of the X-litter normal dogs were bred to each other and produced 100 percent palpation-normal pups, all but one of which were certified, the exception being considered near-normal. These pups, by the way, lost nothing in ability; they were reported to be very good field trial dogs. This brings up an important point: in the early 1960's some breeders felt that breeding for good hips meant sacrificing some other qualities. While such is possible, and there are good reasons to keep the total dog in mind when considering hips, there is no reason why one can't keep breed type and soundness in movement while he eradicates hip dysplasia from his lines. Besides the owners of the field trial retrievers mentioned above, many others have discovered this. One is a noted breeder of Poodles who, along with freedom from dysplasia, has eliminated avascular necrosis despite a high incidence previously, and now finds no slipped patellas and no deviation of the tibial crest with bowing of the humerus and tibia, problems common in Poodles and not unknown in this man's kennel.[44] Breeding for good hips gave that man really good conformation dogs; nothing was lost and health was improved. When they say you can't have the best of two worlds, it isn't true. Or maybe it's really just *one* world, with defective hip genes being chemically related to other defects deep down in the cell where DNA molecules are replicating.

---

*An OFA designation used prior to 1974.

Chapter 14
Summary
and Epilogue

Canine hip dysplasia is a hereditary, developmental condition of the coxo-femoral joint, which may or may not be accompanied by generalized osteochondrosis, but which is generally distinguished by instability expressed in terms of luxation or laxity, abnormal structure in the joint, and degenerative joint disease (arthritis).

This has been an attempt to define and describe the characteristics of the lesions, discuss techniques used in diagnosis and prediction, review its prevalence in various breeds, and present theories on its causes.

We have seen that it is possibly true that "oversupplementation and/or rapid growth have been proposed but not proven experimentally in the etiology of hip dysplasia,"[30] and certainly true that such *does* have great influence on dogs genetically predisposed to the disorder.

I have further presented unproven theories regarding the control or minimization of dysplasia symptoms and severity in the genetically predisposed dog, in the belief that while many may be far from adequately tested, they are deserving of attention if only to stimulate additional ideas and research. Various accepted treatments of the dysplastic dog have been described by Dr. Riser in his contributed chapter.

One writer in a British journal[47] said, "Today we certainly know a little more but we also know that we need to know a lot more and that, as our knowledge increases, we still find that a lot of the information we possess is contradictory." Others sound a bit more optimistic. There is, however, a lot of work to be done and there are many questions which could still be better answered.

Personal Recommendations

It has been said that no one really believes what he has not personally seen or otherwise experienced, and in more than a dozen years of active breeding and research into the field of hip dysplasia before publication of this book, as well as a part-time career in professional handling which has given me much opportunity to examine others' breeding programs, I have reached certain conclusions. These I have tried to save largely for this epilogue, since my intention was to first present as unbiased and impartial a view of the subject as my experience and observations would allow. In deference to the urging of many veterinarians and breeders with whom I have worked, and to satisfy my own urge to make a declaratory statement on what I feel is the key to a good breeding program regarding hips, the following is "Lanting's List," or "Fred's Formula":

Step One: Choose the breed, the type, and the family line(s) that appeal to you. Have another as a stand-by or alternate.

Step Two: Determine which possible brood bitches and stud dogs have the best gene pool. Even if you have to pay for it yourself, get as much information as you can on hip status of not only those dogs directly intended for use in your program, but also their siblings, parents, and grandparents. Wedge radiographs after the age of four months and palpation prediction after eight or ten weeks old will add truly vital statistics to your data bank, especially if you are buying a young dog or have the chance to test the progeny of an older one you may buy.

Step Three: Breed only good dogs with normal hips in all three aspects (palpation, standard, and wedge radiographs). If not feasible in the first generation, at least breed those with the best hips and promise yourself you'll be much stricter the next generation.

Step Four: Feed normally, without fear of inducing hip dysplasia, but do not supplement with calcium. Palpate at 8 to 12 weeks (make your buyers wait). Destroy any with

Grade 2 predictions or worse (more than 2 mm laxity in pups of medium to large breeds); you won't need to put any down the next generation. Cull from your breeding program the predicted Grade 1's (0.5 to 2 mm laxity) and sell them as non-breeding pets, without papers or guarantee if possible. Tattoo with litter letter and number, or AKC number.

Step Five: Wedge-radiograph and palpate at around six months any pups you've kept as possible breeding animals. Tattoo if you haven't already done so. Cull from your program any dogs with unacceptable laxity, however demonstrated.

Step Six: Breed your palpated-normal, wedge-radiographed-normal, OFA-certified dogs to others which have met the same requirements, whether from your own kennel or someone else's. Be careful not to double up or linebreed on any other polygenic defects such as poor temperament, or high rear. Do not worry about simple Mendellian recessives in your first breedings, since color, pattern, coat length, and such can be covered up in one generation and practically removed in two or three when presumably homozygous dogs with desirable dominant traits are bred to.

Step Seven: Stick to it. Always keep the goal in mind and resist temptation to stray from your course.

SECTION V
Other Orthopedic Disorders

Chapter 15
Osteochondrosis—
A Growing Problem
to Dog Breeders *

by Sten-Erik Olsson, V.M.D., Ph.D., M.D.

Most breeders have had the unpleasant experience that skeletal disorders, genetic or nutritional in origin, are common in growing dogs. The majority of skeletal lesions in young dogs affect the joints. Hip dysplasia, Legg-Perthes disease, elbow dysplasia (ununited anconeal process), luxation of the patella and osteochondritis dissecans of the shoulder are well-known such conditions. There are some lesions which do not primarily involve the joints. Panosteitis is located to the shaft of the long bones; hypertrophic osteodystrophy and so-called retained cartilage affect the growth centers of the bones.

Because of its high incidence, hip dysplasia remains the problem of greatest concern to most breeders. In recent years, however, osteochondritis dissecans has become a problem of almost equal concern, at least to breeders of dogs of certain breeds. The main reason is that osteochondritis dissecans has been found with increasing frequency in joints other than the shoulder (Olsson, 1975 a.b.).** Other findings have contributed to a surge of interest in osteochondritis dissecans, its cause, prevention and treatment. A new lesion of the elbow joint called ununited coronoid process or fragmentation of the coronoid process was recently described (Olsson, 1974, 1976). This lesion was found to be of the same nature as osteochondritis dissecans. Several other lesions such as ununited anconeal process and retained cartilage, previously considered to be separate entities, also were shown to be of the same nature.

---

*This chapter originally appeared in the summer 1976 Gaines Progress, and is one of several papers presented at the Gaines Dog Research Center's Seminar, March 14, 1976.

**References mentioned in this chapter are listed at its conclusion.

The findings in dogs together with the results of studies in pigs (Reiland, 1975), horses (Stromberg & Rejno, 1976, Rejno & Stromberg, 1976), turkeys (Poulos, 1976), and broilers (Reiland, et al., 1976) have provided ample evidence that osteochondritis dissecans and the above-mentioned other lesions are manifestations of a generalized skeletal condition called osteochondrosis.

The aim of this paper is to define and describe osteochondrosis and to discuss why it occurs. Clinical appearance and pathology of the various manifestations are reported and the possibility of prevention and treatment discussed.

Normal Growth and Ossification of the Skeleton

Osteochondrosis and its various manifestations cannot be understood without knowledge of the mechanism of skeletal development. Hence this short review.

With the exception of some of the bones of the skull which are formed directly from connective tissue, all the bones of the dog are made of cartilage before they are ossified. Ossification, i.e., formation of bone tissue, does not begin until rather late in fetal life (approximately three to four weeks prior to birth). Ossification begins at certain sites which are called ossification centers. Once ossification has begun, it proceeds in a specific pattern. At the time of birth, most bones in the body are at least partly ossified. In the long bones, the shaft (diaphysis) is ossified, while in many of the long bones the ends (epiphyses) are still cartilaginous but become ossified during the first four months of life. From then on, ossification in the epiphysis, as in the diaphysis, is strictly a part of the process of growth.

Every bone in the body is growing both in length and in width. In order to keep its preformed shape, i.e., a tibia remains a tibia and a femur remains a femur, etc., the bone is being remodeled as it grows. At certain sites, bone resorption therefore dominates over bone formation (Fig. 15-1).

There are certain parts of the bones which remain cartilaginous up to the time when growth is completed. These parts are responsible for most of the longitudinal growth of a bone. They are called metaphyseal growth plates and consist of several layers of cartilage cells. At one side of the growth plate (the one towards the epiphysis) the cells multiply and grow in columns towards the diaphysis. As the cartilage cells reach the diaphyseal side of the growth plate, they have become vesiculated and their intercellular

substance is calcified. At the same time some of the calcified cartilage is removed by cells from the bone marrow and in this way
channels are opened into which vessles penetrate. Bone forming
cells then start to lay down bone on the walls of the channels in
the cartilage. This process, which is a combination of growth,
degeneration, and calcification of cartilage, followed by bone formation continues up until the time when the growth of the dog is
completed. The same process goes on in the joint cartilage, which
is the growth cartilage of the epiphysis. Hence as long as the
animal is growing the joint cartilage has the dual function of being
a protective surface to the bone and simultaneously a growth zone
of the epiphysis (Fig. 15-1).

The kind of bone formation which has been described here is
called endochondral ossification (formation of bone via cartilage).

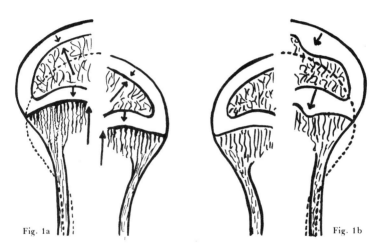

Fig. 1a   Fig. 1b

**Fig. 15-1. a) Schematic diagram of normal growth of epiphysis (top) and
metaphyseal part of the diaphysis (bottom) of a long bone that has flared
extremities. (Bone tissue is striated in diagram.) Short arrows indicate direction of growth of joint cartilage and of metaphyseal growth plate. Long
arrows indicate direction of bone growth in ossified nucleus of the epiphysis and of the metaphyseal part of the diaphysis. The diagram illustrated
(dotted line) how the bone is being remodeled as it grows.
b) Schematic diagram of abnormal growth of a similar bone as in "a."
Because of disturbed endochondral ossification a part of the joint cartilage
and of the metaphyseal growth plates have become thicker than normal
(retained cartilage). In the joint cartilage this is the stage that precedes
osteochondritis dissecans.**

Definition of Osteochondrosis and Osteochondritis Dissecans

The basic feature of osteochondrosis is a disturbance of endo-chondral ossification. The name osteochondrosis means *degeneration of bone and cartilage*. The name is slightly misleading as the lesion is primarily located to the cartilage and only secondarily affects bone. However, the name has been widely accepted and should therefore be used in the future.

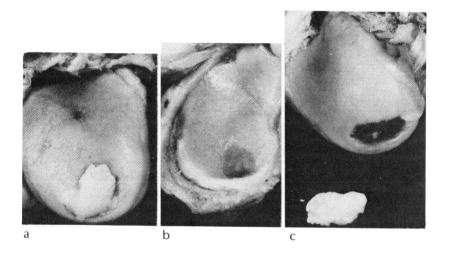

a   b   c

Fig. 15-2. German Shepherd Dog, male, 7 months old. The dog was one in , litter of 9, of which 6 were destroyed because of severe hip dysplasia and osteochondrosis.

a) The figure shows the macroscopic appearance of osteochondritis disse-cans of the right humeral head. There is a large flap of whitish cartilage with a pedicle to the left.

b) Opposing joint surface of the scapula with large erosion, corresponding to the flap of the humeral head.

c) Left humeral head with osteochondritis dissecans. There is a large defect with one small bud of cartilage in the floor of the defect. The bud is a sign of beginning regeneration and scar formation. On the bottom of the pic-ture is a large, thick, loose body (joint mouse) of irregular shape and white color.

In osteochondrosis, the cartilage of the joints and of the growth plate becomes thicker than normal because ossification does not take place in a normal way (Fig. 15-1). As the cartilage continues to grow without being resorbed normally, it becomes necrotic (dies) in its deepest layer. Cracks and fissures occur, particularly in the joint cartilage, which is exerted to the stress of joint movement (Figs. 15-2, 3, 4, 5, 6). Once a crack extends to the surface of the cartilage, synovial fluid gets into the crack and reaches subchondral bone and bone marrow (Fig. 15-6). Likewise, material from the dead cartilage gets into the joint fluid and out into the joint cavity. This may be one reason osteochondrosis causes inflammation in the joint. When osteochondrosis has caused these changes in a joint the lesions are called osteochondritis dissecans. It is called osteochontritis because there is now an obvious inflammatory reaction and dissecans because the fissure dissects away a piece of cartilage which forms a flap or loose body (Fig. 15-2). The flap or loose body (joint mouse) gives rise to a superficial erosion of the cartilage of the opposing joint surface and this also contributes to an inflammatory reaction in the joint.

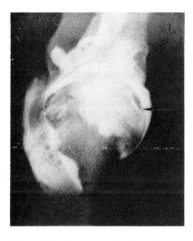

Fig. 15-3. German Shepherd Dog, male, 8 months old. The dog was lame in the left foreleg for about 2 months, when it was first radiographed. A defect was found in the humeral head on plain radiographs of the left shoulder. The figure shows an arthrogram of the shoulder joint and it demonstrates a large cartilage flap. The flap is seen as a dark streak surrounded by the contrast medium in the caudal part of the humeral head (arrow).

Why Does Osteochondrosis Occur?

As mentioned earlier, osteochondrosis has been studied in many species of animals. Reiland's studies in the pig (1975) are of special interest in regard to why and how osteochondrosis develops. Reiland found that osteochondrosis has a very high incidence in the pig and osteochondritis dissecans was found to occur in almost all joints. By intensive selection for fast growth, the pig has been made one of the most rapid-growing of our domestic animals. Reiland demonstrated experimentally that incidence and severity of osteochondrosis was directly related to rapid growth. He showed that osteochondrosis did not occur in pigs that were growing at a lower rate than "normal."

It is interesting to put these experimental findings in the pig in relation to what is known about the incidence of osteochondrosis in a large number of dogs seen by the present author. In nearly 300 cases of osteochondrosis only exceptional dogs were not of medium or larger size. There were twice as many males as females

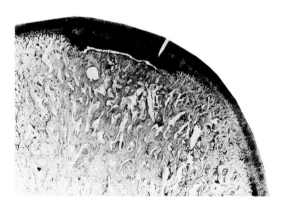

Fig. 15-4. German Shepherd dog, male, 6½ months old, euthanized because of severe hip dysplasia. Multiple changes of osteochondrosis were found at necropsy. There was an area of whitish articular cartilage in the humeral head bilaterally but no visible fissure. The histologic section of the right humeral head showed an early stage of osteochondritis dissecans. The longitudinal fissure in the thickened and degenerated cartilage has not extended to the surface of the joint cartilage. The underlying bone marrow is fibrotic and there also is cyst formation. (The vertical crack in the cartilage is an artifact.)

in these cases and this difference may be explained by the fact that male dogs usually are more rapidly-growing than female dogs. There is probably a hereditary predisposition for osteochondrosis in the dog. A higher incidence of osteochondrosis was found in offspring of certain dogs and there were litters in which all or nearly all puppies were affected. This is in accordance with the findings in pigs by Grondalen & Vangen (1974), and in horses by Rejno & Stromberg (1975).

Nutrition seems to be a factor of importance for the occurrence of osteochondrosis. Hedhammer, et al., (1974) demonstrated experimentally in dogs that overfeeding leads to skeletal changes very similar to those seen in spontaneous osteochondrosis. These authors suggested also that overfeeding of calcium could lead to osteochondrosis. Reiland's nutritional experiment in pigs provided little support for this theory, as high or low calcium feeding did not change the incidence of osteochondrosis. High caloric intake was found to be the main nutritional factor in etiology of osteochondrosis in the pig.

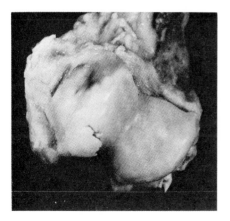

Fig. 15-5. Collie male, 4 months old, euthanized because of osteochondrosis. The figure shows the distal humerus with osteochondritis dissecans of the media condyle. There is a large cartilage flap.

In conclusion, one could say all that is known at the present time indicates dogs with a genetic capacity for fast growth and "pushed" nutritionally (overfed) during their most active growth period stand the greatest risk of developing osteochondrosis.

The Various Manifestations of Osteochondrosis, Their Cause and Development

If it is true that osteochondrosis is a generalized condition, why are there certain predilection sites for its various manifestations? What are the characteristics of these sites? To answer these questions is imperative for the understanding of why and how the various manifestations of osteochondrosis develop.

By studying the normal growth pattern of the skeletons of 19 puppies of two litters and by following the development of the various manifestations of osteochondrosis in about 50 dogs, the present author has arrived at the following conclusion: the various manifestations of osteochondrosis are found where growth is accentuated and where the joint cartilage remains thick up until an age of four or five months. The following examples can be given: the most active growth plate in the body is the one in the distal ulna. The growth plate develops so-called retained cartilage more often and to a higher degree than do other growth plates.

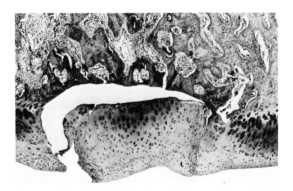

Fig. 15-6. Golden Retriever female, 7 months old, euthanized because of osteochondrosis and hip dysplasia. The histologic section of the medial condyle of the left humerus shows osteochondritis dissecans with a flap of thickened and degenerated cartilage. There is also fibrosis of the bone marrow.

Osteochondritis dissecans of the shoulder joint is almost exclusively located to the caudal portion of the femoral head. This is the part of the head where the joint cartilage remains thicker than in other parts up until the age of four or five months.

In the elbow joint, three locations are prone to develop manifestations of osteochondrosis. These are the craniomedial part of the coronoid process, the anconeal process and the medial condyle of the humerus. The first two structures do not ossify until at an age of about four months, when all other parts of the ulna have ossified except the growth plates. The medial condyle of the humerus, which is a common site of osteochondritis dissecans, retains a thick joint cartilage for a longer period than the lateral condyle of the humerus.

In the femur, osteochondritis dissecans occurs in the condyles (usually the lateral). Osteochondritis dissecans is not seen in the femoral head. One of the differences between the condyles and the femoral head is that ossification proceeds more rapidly in the latter. When the femoral head is ossified and only covered by a rather thin joint cartilage, the condyles still have a long way to go before their ossification is completed. As in other predilection sites of osteochondrosis, the earliest sign of osteochondrosis in the femoral condyles always occurs before ossification is completed. A critical period is the age of four or five months. Radiographically, a defect is seen in the contour of the bone and the reason for this is that ossification has not proceeded at a normal pace at this spot.

There is little question that mechanical factors are of importance for the occurrence of osteochondritis dissecans. Trauma may be a trigger mechanism but osteochondritis dissecans does not occur solely because of trauma.

Osteochondritis dissecans has been often misinterpreted as a result of osteonecrosis (death of bone) or of an osteochondral (bone and cartilage) fracture. These causes of osteochondritis dissecans were not seen in the dog by the present author. They were neither demonstrated in the pig (Reiland, 1975) nor in the horse (Rejno & Stromberg, 1976). Those who have supported the theories that osteochondrosis in animals is caused by osteonecrosis or osteochondral fractures apparently have been misled by observations made in human radiology or during surgery on human patients. There are many conflicting ideas about what causes osteochondritis dissecans in man and more research is needed to settle the conflict. It is the feeling of the present author that studies of osteochondrosis in animals may help to shed light on the problem in man.

One reason osteochondral fractures have been considered to cause osteochondritis dissecans is that bone tissue is often found in the flap or loose body, at least in man and the horse. To explain the presence of bone in a loose body, one has chosen to think that bone and cartilage were ripped off together. There is, however, a better explanation at hand. The piece of cartilage which is dissected away from its normal location is for some time connected to bone or ligament by a strand of connective tissue, and in this way vascularization and bone can be formed. In osteochondritis dissecans at the three most common sites in the dog (the humeral head, the medial condyle of the humerus and the femoral condyles), ossification of the flap does not occur. Only occasionally can ossification be seen in a loose body, if it has adhered to the synovial membrane and thereby become vascularized. Most loose bodies (joint mice) die, disintegrate and disappear after some time; but some survive, grow in the synovial fluid and eventually calcify. In contrast to osteochondritis dissecans of the above-mentioned joints, osteochondritis dissecans of the medial ridge of the talus of the dog often has a flap, which is ossified. This flap is always connected to the collateral ligament and/or the joint capsule. The anconeal process and the medial part of the tip of the coronoid process never do separate completely from the ulna. They are connected to the ulna by a strand of ligament or fibrous tissue; are therefore well vascularized and always contain bone.

Clinical and Radiological Findings in Osteochondrosis

The shoulder joint

For a long time, osteochondritis dissecans was known to exist in the dog only in the shoulder joint. It was first recognized in the 1950's (Schnelle, 1954; Brass, 1956), and a large number of papers have appeared on the subject. Osteochondritis dissecans of the shoulder joint is seen in all large and medium size dogs, predominantly in males. The first clinical signs usually are noticed between the ages of four to seven months. Lameness, insidious in onset on one or both forelegs, which gets worse after exercise, is the most prominent sign. Stiffness after rest is another important sign. Pain usually can be elicited by palpation, flexion, and extension of the shoulder. The clinical signs may vary in severity over periods of weeks or months.

The definite diagnosis is made by radiographic examination. A mediolateral radiograph of the extended shoulder joint usually reveals a defect in the subchondral bone of the humeral head. In mild or early cases, only a flattening of the dorsocaudal contour of the humeral head is seen. It is imperative that the radiographs are of good quality. Sedation or anethesia is necessary as a rule. With the side to be radiographed towards the table, the dog is placed on the cassette. The affected leg is pulled in a cranioventral direction and the opposite leg is pulled caudally out of reach of the well collimated X-ray beams.

In dogs with advanced lesions, there usually is sclerosis of the subchondral bone and sometimes calcification of the cartilage flap which covers the defect. In many cases, the defect is located slightly to the caudolateral instead of the caudal side of the humeral head. Hence, a radiograph made in lateral projection does not visualize the lesion as a defect in the contour of the bone, but rather as an area of decreased density in the caudal part of the head. It should be remembered that the lesion in most cases is bilateral and for this reason both shoulders always should be radiographed, even if there is no history or sign of bilateral lameness.

It usually is easier to make the diagnosis of osteochondritis dissecans of the shoulder joint than to decide what kind of therapy to use. The simple reason is that many cases of osteochondritis dissecans of the shoulder heal spontaneously. The pedicle of the cartilage flap may rupture and the flap become dislodged (Fig. 15-2). Eventually this flap, now turned into a joint mouse, is resorbed by the joint fluid through enzyme activity. Sometimes the natural course is entirely different. The flap remains intact and as long as it covers the floor of the defect, no outgrowth of scar tissue will take place. It is not unusual to find that a lesion in the humeral head on one side heals spontaneously, while the one in the humeral head of the other leg continues to cause problems.

Because the animals show pain and lameness, restriction of exercise has been recommended as part of treatment by many investigators. In contrast, the present author is of the opinion that a dog with osteochondritis dissecans of the shoulder should be allowed to move around as much as possible because in this way the chance is greater that the flap will be dislodged. If necessary, the dog can be given analgesics. If there is no obvious improvement after four to six weeks, surgery should be seriously contemplated. If one can prove the presence of a calcified flap or piece of cartilage in the defect, surgery should be done with no further delay. Even in cases in which the signs are not severe or may have subsided, it is safe to do a repeat radiographic examination. If the radiographs reveal that bone has not filled the defect, an arthrogram should be made to demonstrate whether or not there is a flap or loose piece of cartilage in the defect (Fig. 15-3). If the arthrogram is positive, surgery is indicated. Surgery is not necessary if there is no loose piece or flap *in the defect*, as healing in this case will take place spontaneously. If there is a joint mouse, it usually is lodged in the ventrocaudal pouch of the joint, where in most cases it does not cause any clinical signs. Eventually it will be digested but it also can remain viable and grow in size. If a joint mouse is lodged in the sheath of the biceps tendon it may give rise to pain and lameness and necessitate an operation.

Surgery consists of removal of the cartilage flap or piece of cartilage lying in the defect and trimming of the edges of the defect. The post-surgical care includes restricted exercise for about four weeks.

The elbow joint

In the very young dog it is sometimes not easy to differentiate between lameness caused by pain in the elbow and pain in the shoulder. It is therefore to be recommended that in doubtful cases both the elbow and the shoulder be radiographed. The radiographic examination is of great importance for the early diagnosis of the lesions in the elbow joint, provided proper technique is used. Two projections are necessary, one mediolateral with the elbow fully flexed; the other anterioposterior with about 30-45 degrees flexion of the elbow. It is sometimes useful to have a second mediolateral view of the elbow, this time only in a few degrees of flexion.

There are three lesions in the elbow joint, all of which are manifestations of osteochondrosis. These lesions are osteochondritis dissecans of the medial condyle of the humerus (Olsson, 1974, 1975, a.a. 1976) (Fig. 15-5, 6), fragmentation of the coronoid process (ununited coronoid process) (Olsson, 1974, 1975, a.b. 1976) (Figs. 15-7, 8), and ununited anconeal process (Cawley & Archibald, 1959) (Figs. 15-9, 10). They are all very important not only because they give rise to lameness in the young dog, but also because they usually lead to severe osteoarthrosis.

The three lesions have a similar clinical appearance, at least in the early stages. The owner of a dog with any of these elbow lesions usually complains that the dog has a stiff gait in the fore-legs the first few minutes after a period of rest. This sign usually is seen when the dog is about four or five months old. True lame-ness is rarely noticed until the dog gets a little older. The lesions are often bilateral. For this reason, the dog gets lame on both forelegs and this is difficult for the owner to observe. The bilateral lameness usually is seen as a slightly stiff, stilted gait of the forelegs which usually are held slightly externally rotated, with the elbows close to the chest. Careful clinical examination reveals some pain in the elbows on extension and sometimes on flexion.

Fig. 15-7. Golden Retriever, male, 3 years old, euthanized because he was vicious. The dog had been slightly lame in the left foreleg for a long period. At necropsy, the reason for the lameness was found to be fragmentation of the coronoid process of the ulna with erosion of the opposing joint surface of the medial condyle of the humerus. The figure shows the coronoid proc-ess and part of the humeral head of the two forelegs. There is an ossicle, covered by cartilage, between the coronoid processes of the left ulna and the head of the left radius. (The leg to the right is the left leg.) There is slight discoloration of the cartilage of the ossicle. The coronoid process of the right ulna is normal.

Radiographic examination of the elbows at the age of four to five months is essential for the diagnosis of one of the three lesions, i.e., the one which seems to be the least common, the ununited anconeal process. The other two lesions of the elbow joint do not give rise to radiographic signs at this age.

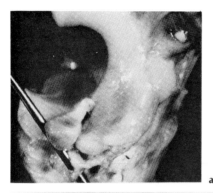

a

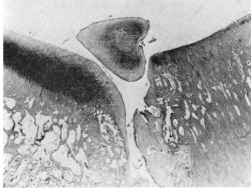

b

Fig. 15-8. German Shepherd Dog, female, 11 months old, euthanized because of hip dysplasia and osteochondrosis.
a) shows the proximal part of the right radius and ulna. There is a large ossicle, covered by cartilage and with an osteophyte on the tip, lying between the coronoid process and the head of the radius. Close to the ossicle is an area of erosion of the joint cartilage of the coronoid process. Small osteophytes are seen on the rim of the coronoid process.
b) Histologic section of the ossicle and the surrounding bone. At the level of this section there is no connection between the ulna (to the right) and the ossicle. Strands of fibrous tissue connected the two structures at a deeper level. There is normal articular cartilag between the ossicle and the radius (to the left). There is severe erosion of the joint cartilage of the coronoid process. The bone is partly denuded.

Ununited anconeal process (elbow dysplasia)

This lesion has long been recognized and it was until recently considered to be the most common cause of osteoarthrosis of the elbow joint. It is found in many breeds of dogs of large size but seems to be a problem mainly in the German Shepherd Dog. There are indications that the condition has a genetic trait because the lesion frequently is found in littermates. Hence, it is not advisable to use a dog with ununited anconeal process for breeding.

In the German Shepherd Dog, the anconeal process ossifies at an age of about 10 to 13 weeks and unites with the rest of the ulna about two to four weeks later. In a normal dog the anconeal process should be united with the ulna, at the latest, at an age of 18-20 weeks. If not united at that time there is little question that the anconeal process will remain ununited. In such a case degenerative changes typical of osteochondrosis, causing cracks and fissures, can be seen histologically in the cartilage between the ossification center and the ulna (Fig. 15-10). The end result usually is a large piece of bone which is only connected with the ulna by a bridge of fibrocartilage or connective tissue.

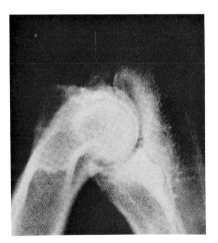

Fig. 15-9. German Shepherd Dog, female, 2½ years old, euthanized because of lameness in the left foreleg, caused by an ununited anconeal process. The radiograph, which was taken in mediolateral projection with the elbo in flexion, shows the ununited anconeal process as a separate ossicle in the joint (arrow). Periarticular osteophytes also can be seen.

Treatment of ununited anconeal process is surgical. The most common procedure is to remove the ununited process via a lateral incision between the lateral epicondyle and the olecranon. It also has been suggested that osteosynthesis should be done, i.e., to screw the process to the ulna in order to avoid the instability which is said to occur when the anconeal process is loose or removed. More research seems to be needed in order to evaluate the result of this kind of treatment. There seems to be a time factor to consider when one decides to do surgery. It is the experience of the present author that surgery should not be done until the dog has reached an age of 9-12 months. If it is done earlier, i.e., during the period of very fast growth (four to eight months), secondary changes (remodeling and osteoarthrosis) seem more likely to develop after surgery than if the ununited anconeal process is left in place until a time when growth is almost completed.

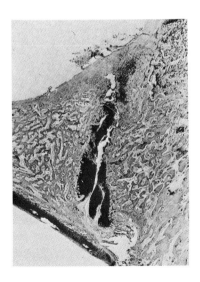

Fig. 15-10. Giant Schnauzer, male, 5 months old, euthanized because of osteochondrosis. The histologic section shows the left anconeal process (to the left), which has not united with the olecranon (to the right). There are fissures in the degenerated cartilage, which lies between the two bones. The picture is typical for the early stage in development of a separate ossicle (ununited anconeal process).

Fragmentation of the coronoid process of the ulna (ununited coronoid process) and osteochondritis dissecans of the medial condyle of the humerus

These two lesions recently were described as cause of osteoarthrosis of the elbow joint and found to be more common than the ununited anconeal process, at least in certain breeds (Olsson, 1975 a.b.). The two lesions are particularly a problem in Golden and Labrador Retrievers but they occur separately or together in most breeds of large dogs.

Fragmentation of the coronoid process seems to be the most common of the two lesions except in the Golden Retriever, in which there is a preponderance for osteochondritis dissecans of the medial condyle of the humerus.

In the early stages the clinical signs of the two lesions are very similar to those of the ununited anconeal process but the radiographic picture is entirely different. As a rule, nothing abnormal can be seen on radiographs before the dog is about seven months of age, although clinical signs may have been present since an age of four to five months. It is therefore imperative to advise the owner of a young dog with slight clinical signs from the elbow joint to return the dog for a repeat radiographic examination four to eight weeks after the first examination. Too many cases hitherto have been missed by veterinarians who have fallen back on the erroneous and diffuse diagnosis of "growing pain." There is no justification for making this diagnosis or, what is even worse, injecting corticosteroids intraarticularly in a young dog, even if the clinical signs are vague and the radiographic picture normal.

The fragmentation of the coronoid process usually cannot be visualized on radiographs. The first radiographic signs instead are small osteophytes on the dorsal aspect of the anconeal process and medially on the coronoid process. The osteophytes on the anconeal process can be seen only if the radiograph is made with the elbow joint in full flexion. If there is a lesion only on one side the diagnosis usually is comparatively easy to make as the difference between the normal and diseased side is obvious, provided one knows what to look for. The differential diagnosis between a case of fragmentation of the coronoid process and a case of osteochondritis dissecans of the medial condyle of the humerus is more difficult. In typical cases of the latter lesion, a small triangular defect can be seen in the weight bearing surface of the medial condyle. This defect often is surrounded by a sclerotic zone.

It is obvious that the two lesions have gone unrecognized up until recently mainly because the early radiographic changes have been overlooked. Once the dog is over a year of age the radiographic signs are obvious and the diagnosis of osteoarthrosis is made. This often means a negative attitude by the veterinarian towards a search for rational treatment as osteoarthrosis (if no obvious cause is found) is considered to be caused by wear and tear.

In the case of fragmentation of the coronoid process and osteochondritis dissecans of the medial condyle of the humerus, surgery preferably should be done as soon as diagnosis is made. Only the medial approach to the elbow joint can be used.

In early cases of osteochondritis dissecans of the medial condyle of the humerus there is a defect in the weightbearing surface, covered by a flap of cartilage (Figs. 15-5, 6). The flap should be removed and the edges of the defect trimmed. In later cases there usually is no flap. Instead it may have been turned into a large, cartilaginous body that may be found adhering to the joint capsule. It may even have been resorbed. In a joint with only a defect and no flap, only the edges of the defect should be trimmed. Whatever the findings the coronoid process should be carefully inspected as osteochondritis dissecans of the medial condyle is frequently combined with fragmentation of the coronoid process. The most common finding in fragmentation of the coronoid process is an elongated, cartilage covered ossicle, which lies between the coronoid process and the head of the radius (Figs. 15-7, 8). Sometimes the coronoid process is fragmented in several small pieces. On the opposing joint surface there always is considerable erosion caused by the loose fragments. All fragments should be removed. After surgery the dog is caged for about 10 days and kept on restricted exercise for a period of four to six weeks. If the only finding at early surgery is fragmentation of the coronoid process and the fragments can be completely removed, prognosis is good. If surgery is done late (after the appearance of large osteophytes), prognosis is guarded. The joint usually will become pain-free but range of motion will remain limited. In cases of osteochondritis dissecans of the humeral condyle or in cases with combination of the two lesions, prognosis always is guarded even if surgery is done early. However, surgery always should be tried as an untreated case of either of the two lesions or a case with the two lesions combined usually develops into a case of very severe osteoarthrosis. It should be remembered, however, that in many dogs with fragmentation of the coronoid process the lesion can remain undetected for years. This usually happens in dogs with bilateral lesions and with owners who are not very observant. These dogs often are first brought to a veterinarian when there is acute lameness due to trauma to one of the severely osteo-arthrotic elbow joints.

The knee (stifle)

Osteochondritis dissecans of the knee (Robins, 1970) is a much more common lesion in dogs of large size than previously assumed (Arbesser, 1974; Olsson, 1975 a.b.). Diagnosis often is difficult to make as the clinical signs in most cases are diffuse in the young dog. The hip joints are apt to be suspected as cause of the lameness rather than the knees. There usually is no obvious lameness; rather a disturbed gait pattern of the hind legs somewhat similar to the "slinky gait" of hip dysplasia. Radiographs are essential for early diagnosis, but only technically good radiographs made in the right projections will reveal a flattening or defect of the lateral or medial condyle. This is true particularly if the lesion is small. A mediolateral radiograph should be made on a cassette with low speed-high resolution screens. Two posterioanterior views with the knee in different angulations should be used. The most common site of a defect is the medial aspect of the weight-bearing surface of the lateral femoral condyle (Figs. 15-11, 12).

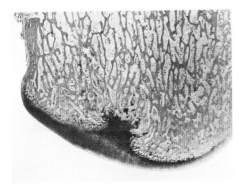

Fig. 15-11. German Shepherd Dog, male, 7½ months old, euthanized because of osteochondrosis; clinically only manifested as an ununited anconeal process. Subclinical changes of osteochondrosis were found in other joints. The histologic section shows the lateral condyle of the left knee. There is an area of retained cartilage, which has not developed into osteochondritis dissecans. The knee joint was otherwise intact.

Many cases of osteochondritis dissecans of the knee remain undetected and heal sometimes only leaving a scar in the condyle. In other cases severe osteoarthrosis develops. Roughly 10-15 percent of all cases of osteoarthrosis of the knee seen in large dogs by the present author are caused by osteochondritis dissecans.

More research has to be done before any definite conclusions can be drawn about why some cases of osteochondritis dissecans of the knee heal without any secondary changes while others give rise to very severe osteoarthrosis. There seems to be no straight-

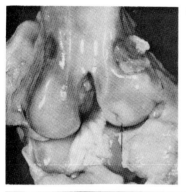

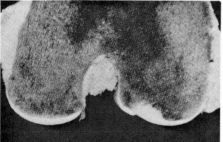

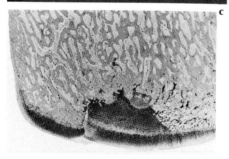

Fig. 15-12. German Shepherd Dog, female, 9 months old, euthanized because of hip dysplasia and osteochondrosis which was only manifested clinically as an ununited anconeal process. The dog was one in a litter of nine, of which all developed ununited anconeal process. On necropsy, osteochondritis dissecans was found in both knees.
a) The opened left knee. Arrow indicated an area of whitish cartilage with a fissure.
b) Two mm thick slab of the knee in "a." At the site of the fissure the cartilage is slightly depressed. The cartilage is thick in the area which was white on the surface.
c) Histologic section of the lateral condyle showing the changes of osteochondritis dissecans. There is retained cartilage which is degenerated in the deepest layer. The fissure is seen to the left.

forward indication for surgery of osteochondrosis of the knee other than in cases with acute lameness, in which the chance is great to find a large flap or a joint mouse. In such cases an exploratory arthrotomy should be done and if a flap or joint mouse is found it should be removed. Once osteoarthrosis has developed there seems to be little one can do to improve the situation other than to give the conventional medical and physical therapy.

The Hock Joint

Osteochondritis dissecans of this joint (Olsson, 1975 a.b.) is not as common as the one in the shoulder, elbow, or knee but common enough to warrant special attention in cases of slight lameness in the hind legs of young dogs. The lesion seems to be particularly common in Labrador and Golden Retrievers but it also does occur in other breeds. The clinical signs usually begin at four to five months of age and are usually very vague. The lesion is more often unilateral than osteochondritis dissecans in other joints. The most typical findings are a slightly shorter step than normal on the affected leg and pain on extension and flexion of the hock. Rather early, the range of flexion is decreased. In some dogs there is obvious joint effusion. As in osteochondritis dissecans of other joints, the radiographic examination provides the diagnosis. The lesion is located to the medial ridge of the talus and is best demonstrated as a defect in this ridge on an anterioposterior film. A fragment often can be seen because it is calcified or ossified. In old cases the fragments can be very large in size. Sometimes a lateral radiograph with the hock joint in as much flexion as possible is useful.

A rather high percentage of loose bodies removed from hock joints contain bone. This is in contrast to osteochondritis dissecans in other joints of the dog, where ossicles are extremely rare.

Surgery is the treatment of choice. By a longitudinal incision caudally to the medial malleolus, the hock joint can be reached. With the leg in flexion the loose bodies easily can be removed. Prognosis is good if surgery is performed early.

The Cervical Intervertebral Joints

Compression of the cervical cord caused by instability of the cervical vertebrae (so-called spondylolisthesis) has been described. It is mostly in Great Danes and in dogs of breeds of similar size.

The reason for instability has remained obscure. The present author has encountered a few cases in growing Great Danes, in which the cause of instability was a lesion in the cranial part of the cranial facets of one or two pairs of intervertebral joints. The lesion had all the criteria of healed osteochondrosis and was very similar to the lesion seen at the same location in pigs. It seemed obvious in these cases of osteochondrosis of the intervertebral joints that the only rational treatment should aim at stabilizing the cervical spine by fusion of some kind.

The Growth Plates

Retained cartilage of various growth plates is seen. In most cases clinical signs are not caused by these changes and usually heal spontaneously. Only advanced lesions in the growth plates of the distal ulna and of the ones of distal femur and proximal tibia seem to give rise to deformation of the legs. In the case of ulna involvement decrease in growth rate of the ulna leads to asymmetry of growth of the ulna and radius. The distal part of the radius is bowed around the distal metaphysis of the slower growing ulna. This leads to lateral deviation of the distal part of the forelimb. When the distal femur and proximal tibia are involved, it usually leads to *genu valgum*. Once there is deformation, surgical correction has to be done but it is safe to wait until growth is completed.

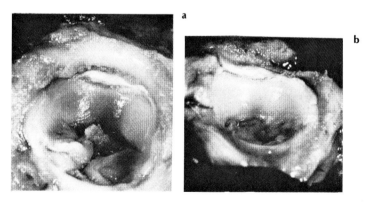

Fig. 15-13. **Golden Retriever, male, 9 months old, euthanized because of osteochondrosis and hip dysplasia.**
a) **The right acetabulum. The joint capsule is thickened and along the dorsolateral rim of the acetabulum is a fissure and an elongated flap of whitish cartilage. The cut round ligament is swollen.**
b) **The left acetabulum. There is a fissure and a flap at the dorsolateral rim.**

It finally should be mentioned that slipped femoral capital epiphysis is a common lesion in osteochondrosis in pigs and there is good reason to suspect that even in the dog slipped epiphysis can be caused by osteochondrosis.

The Role of Osteochondrosis in Hip Dysplasia

The relationship between osteochondrosis and hip dysplasia deserves special mention.

It is well established that hip dysplasia is a developmental condition of multifactorial etiology. The overwhelming number of cases of hip dysplasia are hereditary of polygenic nature. Heritability is about 0.3 (30 percent), which means that environmental factors are of importance for the development of the condition (Larsen, 1973). Rapid growth and development are related to hip dysplasia (Riser, et al., 1964; Lust, et al., 1973; and Olsson & Kasstrom, 1973). It recently was shown that rapid growth caused by overfeeding increased incidence and severity of hip dysplasia in dogs with a hereditary trait for the condition (Kasstrom, 1975). The mechanism by which nutritionally induced rapid growth rate increased incidence and severity of hip dysplasia has, however, remained obscure. When studying the development of the acetabulum in normal and dysplastic hip joints of 24 young dogs, the present author made the following observation: in nearly all the hip joints which became dysplastic in this series, a longitudinal fissure was seen in the cartilage of the dorsolateral rim of the acetabulum (Fig. 15-13). On the opposite joint surface of the femoral head, the cartilage was eroded.

The striking similarity between these findings and osteochondritis dissecans as it appears in other joints (fissures, formation of a flap and erosion of the opposite joint surface) prompted a careful histological study of the pathological changes. The result was unequivocal. The changes at the rim of the acetabulum were the same as in osteochondritis dissecans of other joints. In the thick cartilage of the rim there was degeneration of the deepest layer and fissures had occurred, leading to formation of one or several flaps (Fig. 15-14). Gustafsson, et al., demonstrated in 1975 that the dorsal acetabular rim remains cartilaginous longer than other parts of the hip joint. Hence, the finding of osteochondritis dissecans at this rim is consistent with the findings by the present author that osteochondritis dissecans occurs where the joint cartilage remains thick for a longer period of time.

Osteochondritis dissecans of the rim of the acetabulum must seriously affect the normal development of the hip joint. The disturbance of endochondral ossification of the rim should lead to a more shallow acetabulum than normal. If osteochondritis dissecans of the dorsolateral rim of the acetabulum is a primary lesion in hip dysplasia, it probably is one of the trigger mechanisms in the vicious circle of remodelling and joint laxity (Olsson & Kasstrom,

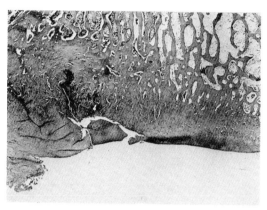

a

b

Fig. 15-14. German Shepherd Dog, male, 8 months old, euthanized because of osteochondrosis and hip dysplasia. The macroscopic changes in the hip joints were similar to those seen in the dog in Fig. 13.
a) Histologic section, showing changes of osteochondritis dissecans at the dorsolateral rim of the acetabulum.
b) Details of "a." A thick joint cartilage with occasional clusters of cells is elevated from the underlying bone and has formed two flaps. There are remnants of necrotic cartilage in the defect.

1973; Riser, 1973). Research into the cause of osteochondrosis therefore must be of great importance also for the understanding of why hip dysplasia occurs. If, on the other hand, osteochondritis dissecans of the acetabulum is only one of the many changes caused by instability of the hip joint, it is nevertheless a finding of interest as it explains why hip dysplasia gets worse if the dog is overfed. Further studies of the relationship between hip dysplasia and osteochondrosis also should shed some light on what role mechanical factors play in the development of osteochondritis dissecans.

There are other connections between hip dysplasia and osteochondrosis than the finding of osteochondritis dissecans of the acetabular rim. A large number of young dogs in the present study, euthanized because of hip dysplasia, were found to have multiple manifestations of osteochondrosis most often not diagnosed clinically. One also should remember that osteochondritis dissecans and hip dysplasia occur with highest frequency in the same kinds of dogs, i.e., large dogs with the critical period being the one of fastest growth between four and eight months. There is one obvious difference, however, between the two conditions.

b

Fig. 15-15. Twelve year old male with ununited anconeal process, a form of osteochondrosis of the elbow.
a) Note "east-west" placement of feet and slight enlargement of elbow, breaking a smooth line from shoulder to lower foreleg.
b) Due to increased discomfort in old age, this dog would recline with elbows touching and one tucked under.

Courtesy F. L. Lanting

While osteochondrosis occurs twice as often in males as in females, hip dysplasia occurs with the same frequency in both sexes.

It is the hope of the present author that the new concept of osteochondrosis as a growth related, generalized condition manifesting itself as osteochondritis dissecans and retained cartilage, will stimulate renewed interest in the genetic, nutritional, endocrinological and metabolic factors which govern the development of cartilage and endochondral ossification.

There is little question that the incidence of osteochondrosis is increasing and that it in one way or the other is related to hip dysplasia, the most common orthopedic disorder in the dog.

Summary

On the basis of nearly 300 cases of osteochondrosis in the dog the author defines the condition and describes the various lesions to which it gives rise. Osteochondrosis in the dog is compared to osteochondrosis in other species and it is concluded that the common denominator is disturbance of endochondral ossification.

Fig. 15-16. Otti von der Erlalohe at 12 years exhibiting correct shoulder and elbow assembly. Note smooth transition from upper to lower foreleg and no turning out of the feet.

Courtesy F. L. Lanting

The most important manifestation of osteochondrosis is osteochondritis dissecans, which begins as a thickening of the joint cartilage with necrosis of its deepest layer. Cracks and fissures occur, thereby dissecting a piece of the cartilage which forms a flap or loose body.

The author describes the natural course of osteochondritis dissecans in several joints, reports the clinical and radiological picture and discusses treatment. He points out that osteochondritis dissecans is much more common in the dog than previously assumed, particularly in the elbow and the knee. Osteochondritis dissecans in the hock joint is slightly different from the lesion in the other joints, as the loose piece often contains bone.

The relationship between osteochondrosis and hip dysplasia is discussed and the author demonstrates that osteochondritis dissecans occurs in the acetabulum of the dysplastic hip joint.

It is concluded that more research is needed into the basic mechanism of endochondral ossification and cartilage metabolism, as well as their dependence on genetic and environmental factors. Such research is important in order to understand why incidence of osteochondrosis is rising in most domestic animals.

Acknowledgements

This investigation was supported by the John M. Olin Foundation and Statens Medicinska Forskningsrad (B76-17x-00645-11A).

References for Chapter 15

1. Arbesser, E. *Osteochondrosis Dissecans der Femurkondylen beim Hund,* Wiener Tierarztl, Mschr., 61:303 (1974).
2. Brass, W. *Uber die Osteochondrosis des Hundes,* Tierarztl Umsch, 11:200 (1956).
3. Cawley, A. J. and Archibald, J. *Ununited Anconeal Process of the Dog,* J. Am. Vet. Med. Ass., 138:454 (1959).
4. Grondalen, T., and Vangren, O. *Osteochondrosis and Anthrosis in Pigs, V., A Comparison of the Incidence in Three Different Lines of the Norwegian Landrace Breed,* Acta vet. scand., 15:16 (1974).
5. Gustafsson, P. O., Olsson, S. E., Kasstrom, H. and Weyyman, B. *Skeletal Development of Greyhounds, German Shepherd Dogs and their Crossbreed Offspring, An Investigation with Special Reference to Hip Dysplasia,* Acta radiol. Suppl, 344:81 (1975).
6. Hedhammer, A., Wu, F. M., Krook, L., Schryver, H. F., de-Lahunta, A., Whalen, J. P., Kallfelz, F. A., Nunez, E. A., Hintz, H. F., Sheffy, B. E. and Ryan G. D. *Overnutrition and Skeletal Disease, An Experimental Study in Growing Great Dane Dogs,* Cornell Vet. 64, Suppl. 5 (1974).
7. Kasstrom, H. *Nutrition, Weight Gain and Development of Hip Dysplasia, An Experimental Investigation in Growing Dogs with Special Reference to the Effect of Feeding Intensity,* Acta radiol. Suppl., 344:136 (1975).
8. Larsen, J. S. (editor) *Symposium Workshop Panel Reports in Canine Hip Dysplasia,* Proc. Canine Hip Dysplasia Symposium and Workshop, St. Louis, MO., p. 158, 1973, (Oct. 19-20, 1972).
9. Lust, G., Geary, J. C. and Sheffy, B. E. *Development of Hip Dysplasia in Dogs,* Amer. J. Vet. Res., 34:87 (1973).
10. Olsson, S. E. *An ny Typ av Armbagsledsdysplasi hos Hund?* (in Swedish), (A new type of elbow dysplasia in the dog?), Sv. Vet. tidn., 26:152 (1974).
11. Olsson, S. E. *Osteochondritis Dissecans in the Dog,* Proc. Amer. Anim. Hosp. Ass. 42nd Ann. Meeting, Proc. Vol. 1:360, Cincinnati, Ohio (1975a).
12. Olsson, S. E. *Lameness in the Dog, A Review of Lesions Causing Osteoarthrosis of the Shoulder, Elbow, Hip, Stifle, and Hock Joints,* Proc. Amer. Anim. Hosp. Ass. 42nd Ann. Meeting, Proc. Vol. 1:363, Cincinnati, Ohio (1975b).

13. Olsson, S. E. *Osteochondrosis of the Elbow Joint in the Dog, Its Manifestations, Indications for Surgery and Surgical Approach,* Submitted for publication to Archives of the American College of Veterinary Surgeons (1976).
14. Olsson, S. E. and Kasstrom, H. *Etiology and Pathogenesis of Canine Hip Dysplasia,* Canine Hip Dysplasia, Proc. Canine Hip Dysplasia Symposium and Workshop, St. Louis, MO., p. 1, 1973 (Oct. 19-20, 1972).
15. Poulos, P. personal communication (1976).
16. Reiland, S. *Osteochondrosis in the Pig,* (Preprint), Acta radiol. 1-118 (1975).
17. Reiland, S., Poulos, P., Hansen, H. J., Lindgren, N. O. and Olsson, S. E. *Osteochondros hos Broiler,* in press (1976).
18. Rejno, S. and Stromberg, B. *Osteochondrosis in the Horse II, Pathology,* (Preprint), Acta radiol., 1-28 (1976).
19. Riser, W. H. *The Dysplastic Hip Joint: Its Radiographic and Histologic Development,* J. Am. Vet. Rad. Soc., 14-35 (1973).
20. Riser, W. H., Cohen, D., Lindqvist, S., Mansson, J. and Chen S. *Influence of Early Rapid Growth and Weight Gain on Hip Dysplasia in the German Shepherd Dog,* J. Am. Vet. Med. Ass. 145-661 (1964).
21. Robbins, G. M. *A Case of Osteochondritis Dissecans of the Stifle Joints in a Bitch,* J. Small Anim. Pract., 11:813 (1970).
22. Schnelle, G. B. *Congenital Dysplasia of the Hip (Canine) and Sequelae,* Proc. 91st Ann. Meeting Am. Vet. Med. Ass., p. 253 (1954).
23. Stromberg, B. and Rejno, S. *Osteochondrosis in the Horse I, A Clinical and Radiologic Investigation of Osteochondritis Dissecans of the Knee and Hock Joint,* (Preprint), Acta radiol., 1-15 (1976).

Chapter 16
The Panosteitis *
Problem

This mysterious disease causes sudden lameness in many younger dogs, but its greatest potential danger may lie in false diagnosis.

One of the main reasons for a young dog to be "pulled" from a show, or excused from the ring, is the sudden lameness or a condition known as panosteitis, familiarly labelled "pano" by many breeders. Of some 130 breeds recognized by the American Kennel Club and similar organizations in other countries, a dozen or less have been reported to be affected.[19]** The disease has been given various names: hematogenic chronic osteomyelitis,[3] enostosis,[6,7,16] long-bone disease, panosteitis,[9] and eosinophilic panosteitis.[15,17,21] It was first described by Gratzl,[9] and Baumann and Pommer[2] in 1951 in Vienna. Since then it has been reported in Sweden,[12] Germany,[8] Hungary, Yugoslavia,[22,23] and the United States,[1,3] yet the search for scientific literature on the subject was not easy: there was no reference in Hungerford's "Diseases of Livestock," Woods' "Diagnostic Orthopaedic Pathology," or the 1977 and 1978 "Index Medicus." Smith's otherwise comprehensive text on Veterinary Pathology had a brief note on enostosis as "a German Shepherd Dog disease," "analogous to eosinophilic panosteitis." An obscure Yugoslavian doctoral thesis[23] dated 1961 led to a couple of references, and a dogged search (pardon the pun) of the international orthopedic literature finally turned up a 1970 study[3] published in the AVMA Journal. Personal contact with orthopedic and radiology specialists[5,11] brought the search to the most recent work at Purdue.[19] For one whom Agatha Christie

---

*Reprinted from the May 1979 issue of Pure-Bred Dogs/American Kennel Gazette, published by the American Kennel Club, New York, NY.

**Refers to references at the end of Chapter 16.

could always keep in the dark until the last page, it was difficult detective work.

Symptoms

Clinical signs, or symptoms, are those which are obvious or apparent upon gross examination of the entire dog, as opposed to microscopic or restricted to a small area. This would include gait and motion analysis, and comparison with other limbs by manipulation and palpation. In humans such signs would include a verbal report by the patient of his complaint. Radiologic study involves the use of X-rays, and histologic determination usually requires euthanasia and dissection of the tissues involved. A similar term, pathologic, also refers to laboratory findings of structural and functional aspects of disease.

Panosteitis is a generalized (pan-) inflammation (-itis) of certain bones (os). Specifically, it occurs in five of the long bones of the appendicular skeleton: the humerus, radius, and ulna of the foreleg, and the femur and tibia of the hindleg. It has not been reported in the long but very narrow fibula of the lower rear leg. More often than not, the first sign is a sudden lameness in one foreleg. Exhibitors have claimed it always occurs after the closing date for show entries, but this has not been scientifically substantiated by unbiased observers.

Intensity of discomfort varies not only with the progression of the lesion in the individual, but with the difference in pain threshhold between one dog and another. It may be so minor that one has to press and probe to elicit pain response, or it may be so bad that the dog will whimper and refuse to put any weight on the limb. The degree of pain is not closely correlated with the progress as observed on radiographs. While lameness may often be observed in only one limb, the disease has been radiographically discovered in at least two bones simultaneously in some 96 percent of affected dogs.[3] Further, the typical lameness-recovery cycle of one or two weeks will shift from one leg to another, although there may actually be as many as seven bones involved at any one time.[19] Usually, a foreleg will be affected first, followed by a hind leg, and often the problem will reappear in one of the forelegs. There might be a lapse of several weeks in between, and more than one phase may be present at any one time in the individual.

Whether the same bone is commonly the site of a recurrence is not a matter of agreement as yet: one study[3] of 100 consecutive cases at New York's Animal Medical Center concluded that "after a bone has passed through all phases of the disease, it is unlikely that it will be affected again," reporting only one incidence of return to a previously affected bone. Another study[19] released five years later held that "recurrence in the same bone was most frequently found in the radius, followed by the ulna . . . ," but mentioned a six-month or more interval between episodes in individual long bones.

Diagnosis

Symptoms of panosteitis may be confused with those of osteochondritis dissecans of the shoulder[17] or ununited anconeal process (commonly but mistakenly referred to as "elbow dysplasia"). The latter is usually brought to light via trauma such as jumping off a ledge and landing on the forelegs, but panosteitis shows up regardless of traumatic occurrences. The most reliable, perhaps the only really definitive diagnosis is made with a series of radiographs which can show the early, middle, and late phases of the disease. Even then, radiographic signs can be so minimal that they can be missed, even if the animal exhibits clinical signs and a number of films are correctly exposed. Radiographs in both major studies[3,19] were taken every month for the period five months to 2½ years of age. Although radiographically panosteitis resembles some human bone conditions, there is no real counterpart in man.[3]

Three Stages

The first phase, the one most associated with acute pain, exhibits the least evidence of the lesion's presence as is evidenced in X-ray photographs. There is some blurring, and an accentuation of the pattern of fibrous bands extending from the cortex (the hard, dense part of the bone) inward to the center of the medullary canal, where the marrow is located. Film contrast between the canal and cortex is diminished, and the densities of the medulla and its lining are slightly greater. The fatty connective tissue takes on an appearance similar to eosinophilic granulomas (hence one of the early names for the disease) and bone is added to those

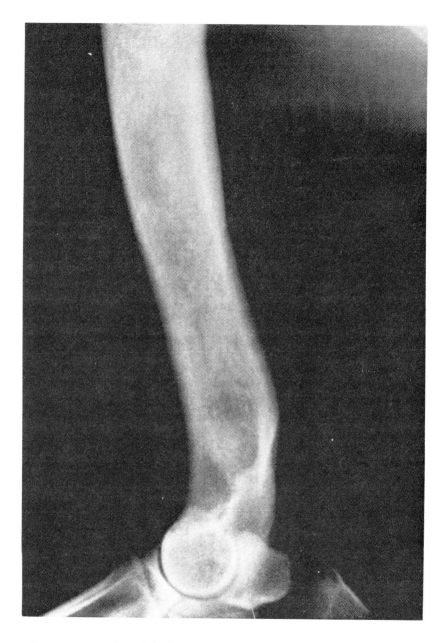

Fig. 16-1. Panosteitis of the humerus (upper forelimb). An increase in endosteal and periosteal bone has decreased the detail of the cortex as the marrow cavity increases in bone density. Compare with Figure 2.

Courtesy J. K. Burt, D.V.M.,
Ohio State University Veterinary Hospital.

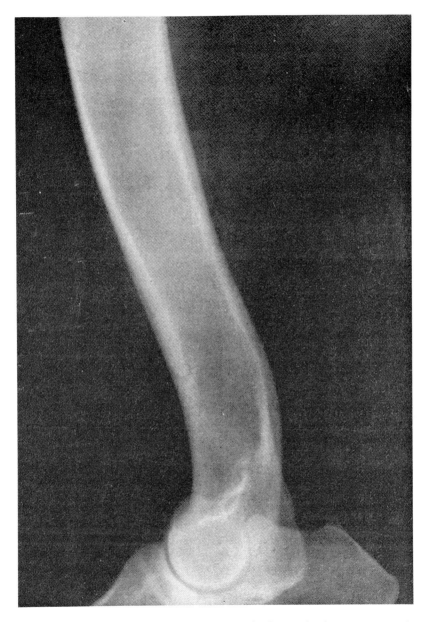

Fig. 16-2. Same bone as Figure 1 two months later. The bone response in the marrow cavity has resorbed giving more contrast with the cortex of the bone. Bone production outside the cortex (periosteal) remains as a thick bone layer along the caudal border.

Courtesy J. K. Burt, D.V.M.,
Ohio State University Veterinary Hospital.

fibrous bands called trabeculae. The great deal of congestion in the medullary canal could be the reason for the early pain. If a hole is drilled (a punch biopsy) for the purpose of testing some of the marrow, pain is abruptly diminished.

The second phase is easily diagnosed by the appearance of radiodense, mottled, medullary tissue, beginning in the vicinity of the nutrient foramen, that hole in the side of the bone where blood vessels enter and leave. The borders of this hole are characteristically accentuated, the cortex appears less dense, and its inner lining becomes roughened. In cases where the medullae are greatly affected, a remodelling (new bone formation) takes place as a secondary response on the cortex's outer layer, the periosteum, growing to several milimeters thick.[5] Such swelling or inflammation of the bone gives panosteitis its present name. In six or eight weeks these characteristics gradually merge into the third phase.

During the approach of the third phase, the fibrous bone that formed in the medullae is resorbed, giving the radiologist a more normal picture again, and production of blood by the marrow resumes a more normal procedure. It may take several months for the bone to regain normal shape especially in the more mature dog, but they generally do heal satisfactorily. Interestingly, no fractures accompanying or following panosteitis which could be considered related have been reported, despite changes in the apparent porosity and density of these organs as found in histopathologic examinations of euthanized dogs. Nor was there any evidence of acute infection or chronic inflammation. The disease and recovery reach a point of cessation, with some evidence of its having been there observable upon dissection and microscopic examination. A little of the marrow seems to be permanently replaced by fibrous connective tissue rather than bone, and the thickening of the outer surface gradually returns toward normal.

Cause

The cause or etiology is unknown, but fortunately the disease is self-limiting: it follows a progressive pattern and the animal recovers with or without treatment to a normal state or one so close you could not tell without removing the bones and slicing them up for the microscope. Since panosteitis is a disease of the fatty bone marrow in the long leg bones of the adolescent or young adult dog, it may be that research on bone marrow will lead to an understanding of the etiology and hence the best treatment, cure, and prevention of panosteitis.

The disease was originally designated as hematogenic chronic osteomyelitis,[2,9,22] associated with fever and infection. More recent work indicates these conditions, when present, are coincidental and not causative. As mentioned earlier, infection is generally not associated, and malignancy is likewise absent. Only one of the 100 dogs in the Animal Medical Center study had tonsillitis. Whenever vaccines, flea powders, worm medicine, diet, and other environmental factors have been implicated, rechecking found that the only common denominator was physiological stress.[19] Bacteriologic cultures of marrow, and the histologic examinations rules out bacterial agents. White blood cell counts and eosinophil counts were within normal in nearly all cases, the rare exceptions being no doubt a result of some co-existing but unrelated problem. An eosinophil is a type of cell of the peripheral blood or bone marrow, and a high level is an indication of some sort of infection or attack by parasites.

Transmission

In an experiment[19] to discover possible genetic, infectious, or contagious modes of transmittal, German Shepherd Dogs with a history of panosteitis were crossed with Pointers from a family in which it had not been observed. Also, purebred Pointers and German Shepherd Dogs were kennelled side by side separated only by a wire fence, and pups of both breeds were raised together in the same pen. Regardless of contact, the Pointers remained free of the disease while the German Shepherd Dogs routinely developed it. The crossbreeding results were inconclusive, even though only one incident of panosteitis showed up as late as the fourth generation of back crossing the female crossbreds to male German Shepherd Dogs.

Panosteitis does not appear to be related in any way to other, radiographically similar diseases. It has no bearing on, nor is it affected by, other bone or joint diseases such as hip dysplasia or osteochondrosis in its various manifestations.

Nutrition possibly has nothing to do with the lesion, though it occurs mostly in large, fast-growing breeds. Calcium intake most likely has no bearing at all, as evidenced in bone healing studies.[11] However, this author has had in his kennel only one case of panosteitis in 140 German Shepherd Dogs, which occurred seven months after the dog was sold to a home where his diet was considerably "richer" than the balanced, commercial dry dog food he was used to. Clinical symptoms ended about ten days after onset, with the administration of prednisone, and no further episodes occurred. A question of nutritional impact upon the disease can be raised when comparing the dog's change in diet with the predominant diet of those in the 100-dog study: raw or cooked beef, eggs, cereal, and milk. Perhaps most of those 100 patients were from "pet" homes where a dog is more likely to be "overnourished." There are other questions which can only be answered through research, but there is no active, current project underway regarding the cause and control of panosteitis.

Treatment

A great number of treatments have been proposed and tried, but all have had success only as palliatives. Since the cause is unknown, only treatment for the symptoms is indicated and routinely prescribed. Aspirin, sulfa compounds, other antibiotics, vitamin C, prednisolone or similar steroids, and calcium supplements have been most commonly used. It appears that aspirin or a substitute less irritating to the canine digestive tract has the greatest effect and the widest application in relieving the pain. Corticosteroids have an anti-inflammatory action and can give remarkable relief, but as in the case of all drugs and foreign substances, the owner of an afflicted dog should ask his veterinarian about the possible side effects and contraindications.

Panosteitis is self-limiting; i.e., it will "go away" whether one treats it or not, and the relief of acute pain without excessive use of palliatives is the only thing that can be done for the dog. One orthopedist[11] said, "It's sort of like treating a cold in a human patient, where if you give medicine it takes about seven days to get over it, and if you do nothing it takes about a week." In the case of this disease, however, it may take anywhere from two days to seven weeks for the pain to leave one site, with one to two weeks quite common. Radiologically and histologically, it can be two months between onset and the beginning of the late phase, and then several more months before cortex and endosteum (inner lining of the marrow cavity) regain normal appearance.[3]

It may take considerably longer for the disease to run its course in all the bones that may become affected. This author has observed that most cases are outgrown by age 18 months to two years, with most initial episodes coming around eight to ten months of age. This is certainly not to say it takes ten or fifteen months for pain and lameness to subside for good, since in many dogs the disease will strike at a much later age than in others. In most cases it's a matter of from ten days to two or three months, with symptoms appearing only intermittently in many. It is rarely a chronic situation in regard to pain, and many dogs will have but one episode. Another, perhaps more accurate, observation showed first diagnosis to be between 5 and 12 months of age in the majority of cases.

Breed, Age, and Sex Correlation

When first described,[2,9] one of the names given the disease was "chronic osteomyelitis of young German Shepherd Dogs," but as it was studied in subsequent years, other breeds were found to be affected, including the Airedale, Irish Setter, German Short-haired Pointer, Doberman Pinscher, Great Dane, Basset Hound, and Saint Bernard. One observer[11] has seen panosteitis in all of the large and giant breeds, but while it is mainly a problem of large dogs, it has also been found in the Miniature Schnauzer and the Scottish Terrier.[9,18,19]

The apparent prevalence in the German Shepherd Dog may be due to the large population of this breed. Only if one considers all three sizes of Poodles as one breed would there be a larger population than German Shepherd Dogs in the United States and Canada. Worldwide, the breed is number one. Clinics, such as the one in which the data[3] on 100 consecutive cases were collected, have a preponderance of German Shepherd Dogs as patients. If the recent trend of Doberman Pinscher registrations being larger than any other breed continues for enough years for the population to approach that of the German Shepherd Dog, it will be interesting to see if the incidence of panosteitis found in private practice and university clinics rises in proportion.

Body size affects the number of cases seen in a veterinary hospital or educational institution. As with hip dysplasia,[14] a greater weight on an affected limb will result in a greater likelihood of clinical signs and therefore more dogs of larger size will be brought to the veterinarian for diagnosis. A lightweight dog, generally speaking, will have less pain and lameness. Incidentally, the Basset Hound is a large dog. It just has short legs.

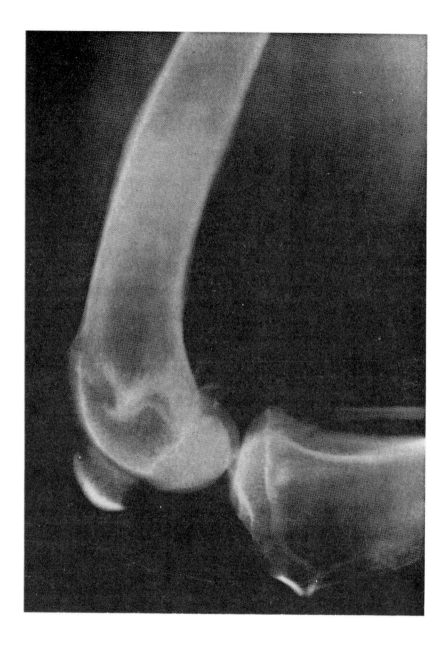

Fig. 16-3. Localized lesion of panosteitis in the femur (thigh bone). The reaction involves bone production inside the marrow cavity (endosteal) and outside the cortex (periosteal). Compare with Figure 4.

Courtesy J. K. Burt, D.V.M.,
Ohio State University Veterinary Hospital.

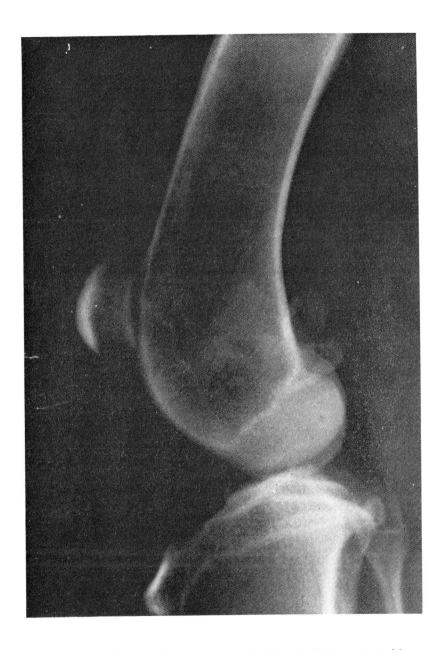

Fig. 16-4. Same bone as Figure 3 two months later. Only the periosteal bone response remains. This bone production becomes remodeled into cortical bone as healing progresses.

Courtesy J. K. Burt, D.V.M.,
Ohio State University Veterinary Hospital.

Growth rate is a possible factor, as it seems to be with hip dysplasia. Most of the large and giant breeds have an early rapid growth pattern which seems to have a bearing on the development of hip joint changes in the two to six month old pup, and it is postulated that there may also be a connection between rate of growth and panosteitis, though the latter is an unproven theory as yet. It is this author's guess that the relatively flatter growth curve in Doberman Pinschers, perhaps inherited from its Greyhound ancestry, will keep incidence of panosteitis in the breed low in proportion to its population. There may be other genetic predisposing factors as well.

If one subtracts the extremes of one case diagnosed at two months of age and one at five years, the curve rises from around five months to peak around ten months, and rapidly diminishes, with very few cases after 18 months of age. In the study[3] previously mentioned, an extraordinary number of cases (ten) were found at age 24 months and appears to be a fluke.

There is close to a four-to-one ratio of males to females affected[3] by panosteitis; the clinical signs are more severe and the disease more chronic in males.[19] This fits a pattern found elsewhere: early in the United States space program it was discovered that women could withstand the stress of G-forces better than men. The United States Army determined that female dogs can run 26 percent longer and swim 46 percent longer than males.[13] Bitches lead many racing teams of sled dogs because they run smoother and calmer, for one reason. And females are much less prone to non-specific lameness according to the records of Zero Kennel;[13] presumably this includes panosteitis. It appears the stress of estrus (bitch's season) or pregnancy contributes[19] somewhat to susceptibility.

Conclusions

In summary, panosteitis is a self-limiting disease affecting many of the long leg bones, predominately in large dogs between five months and one to two years in age. It is apparently unrelated to other lesions of the blood or skeletal systems, and occurs only in the canine. The cause or causes are unknown, and no completely satisfactory connection has been drawn to either genetic transmission or environmental factors such as nutrition, though there is food for thought and experimentation in those areas. It is unlikely much research funding will be made available for panosteitis, since afflicted individuals "outgrow" the disease with usually only minor or occasional need for analgesic or other treatment. The dog owner is advised to consult his veterinarian for confirmation of a "home diagnosis" in order to rule out other problems. Most symptoms of panosteitic dogs will be sufficiently different from those of dogs with osteochondrosis or dysplasia for the average well-read breeder and many other owners to identify the disease correctly.

References and Additional Bibliography for Chapter 16

1. Barrett, R. B., Schall, W. D. and Lewis, R. E. *Diagnosis of Eosinophilic Panosteitis,* J.A.A.H.A., 4:94-104 (1968).
2. Baumann, R. and Pommer, A. *Chronic Osteomyelitis of Young (German) Shepherd Dogs,* Wein, Tierarztl Mschr., 38:670-676 (1951).
3. Bohning, R. H., Jr., Suter, P. F., Hohn, R. B. and Marshall, J. *Clinical and Radiologic Survey of Canine Panosteitis,* J.A.V.M.A. 156:870-883 (1970).
4. Burt, J. K. and Wilson, G. P. *A Study of Eosinophilic Panosteitis (Enostosis) in German Shepherd Dogs,* Acta Radiolog. (Stockh.) Suppl., 319:7-13 (1972).
5. Burt, J. K. personal correspondence.
6. Cotter, S. M., Griffiths, R. C. and Leav, I. *Enostosis of Young Dogs,* J.A.V.M.A., 153:401-410 (1968).
7. Evers, W. H. *Enostosis in a Dog,* J.A.V.M.A., 154:799-803 (1969).
8. Gartner, K. *Klinische Beobachtugen an der Eosinophilen Panostitis der Junghunde,* Kleitierpraxis, 1:71-75 (1956).
9. Gratzl, E. *Die Eosinophile Panostitis der Junghunde,* Wein, Tierarztl Mschr., 38:629-670 (1951).
10. Hardy, W. D., Jr. and Stockman, W. S. in *Clinico-Pathologic Conference,* J.A.V.M.A., 154:1600-1608 (1969).
11. Hohn, R. B. personal correspondence.
12. Kasstrom, H., Olsson, S. E. and Suter, P. F. *Panosteitis in the Dog,* Acta Radiolog. (Stockh.) Suppl., 319 (1972).
13. Kronfeld, D. S. *Home Cooking for Dogs, Part IX,* Pure Bred Dogs-American Kennel Gazette, pp. 50-55 (Nov. 1978).
14. Lanting, F. L. *Hip Dysplasia, Cause and Control.* Dog World (Sept. 1978 and further installments).
15. Riedesel, D. H. *Eosinophilic Panosteitis of Young Dogs,* Iowa State Univ. Vet., 31:29-33 (1969).

16. Smith, Veterinary Pathology, pp. 1073-1074.
17. Sprinkle, T. A. and Krook, L. *Hip Dysplasia, Elbow Dysplasia, and "Eosinophilic Panosteitis," Three Clinical Manifestations of Hyperestrinism in the Dog,* Cornell Vet., 60:476-490 (1970).
18. Tandy, J. and Haywood, S. *A Case of Panosteitis,* Vet. Rec. 100:287-289 (1977).
19. Van Sickle, D. C. "Canine Panosteitis," in *Selected Orthopedic Problems in the Growing Dog,* A.A.H.A., pp. 20-28, South Bend, IN (1975).
20. Wamberg, K. *Atlas Radiologica,* 1st ed., Medical Book Co., Copenhagen, Denmark, p. 378 (1966).
21. Whorton, S. *Eosinophilic Panosteitis in the Dog,* Amer. J. Vet. Clin. Path. 2, pp. 241-244 (1968).
22. Zeskov, B. *A Contribution to "Eosinophilic Panosteitis" in Dogs,* Zentralbl. Vet. Med. 7:671-680 (1960).
23. Zeskov, B. *Prelog Eosinofilnom Panestitisu U. Njemackih Ovcara* (Doctoral Thesis), Zagreb. (1961).

Chapter 17
Hypertrophic
Osteodystrophy (HOD)   *

HOD is a painful, crippling disease of the long bones of the legs in medium, large and giant breeds. This chapter reports on the latest research on this disturbing illness.

The Boxer pup the Smiths bought was a very promising individual with a great pedigree. Here, they hoped, was the foundation of their successful showing and breeding future. But in a matter of a couple of weeks, a previously unnoticed cowhocked condition developed and worsened. They shrugged this off, having heard that dogs with "extreme" rear angulation sometimes develop loose hocks between two and six months of age. The pup will outgrow it, they thought.

But in another month the new pup was acting sickly, evidencing an uncharacteristic listlessness. Rectal temperature showed a fever, and because the pup had intermittant diarrhea, it was started on antibiotics. (It had already been routinely treated for worms even though there were no eggs or spores in recent stool checks.) A week later the pup "went down" with partial paralysis in the rear, and very weak pasterns with splayed feet and swollen "wrists" or carpal-foreleg joints.

There followed a succession of treatments; Mediprin, Bufferin, Prednisolone, antibiotics, Vitamin D, calcium gluconate, Vitamin C, etc. Sometimes it seemed one course of action was working when suddenly the condition would worsen. Months of worry, pity, temporary relief of pain, nursing care, and assistance passed before the pup pulled out of this perplexing condition. Never did it attain the stature and weight of most others of its breed and line, nor did it lose its cowhocked stance and gait, but it finally gained normal health.

---

*Reprinted from the March 1980 issue of Pure Bred Dogs/American Kennel Gazette, published by the American Kennel Club.

Many variations on the above theme have been played by a frustrating and painful disease known as "HOD," or hypertrophic osteodystrophy. Hyper- means excessive, trophy or trophic refers to growth, and os or osteo- refers to bones. Since the excessive bony growth around the shaft of affected bones does not always occur, the term "metaphyseal osteopathy" has been suggested, after the portion of the bone most affected.

Breed and Age Correlation

Once thought to be strictly a problem in giant breeds, HOD has also been seen in many large and medium size breeds, most recently including Setters, Labrador Retrievers, Doberman Pinschers, Weimeraners, Pointers, German Shepherd Dogs, Collies, Boxers, Basset Hounds, Great Danes, and Borzoi. Perhaps the greatest occurrence has been reported in Irish Setters. It appears that early rapid growth rate is a factor,[15]** as it is in the case of hip dysplasia[7,14] and possibly in panosteitis,[8] but size of the individual does not play any role.[3]

One Greyhound, 20 months old, was diagnosed in Sydney, Australia as suffering from HOD, but because of its untypical age and probably track diet, it may possibly have been something else.[17] One group of researchers[9] in 1975 gave the age range as three to eight months, but a 1973 study[17] reported an eight-week old pup which had symptoms for two weeks before being presented at the clinic. A four-year Norwegian compilation of 26 affected dogs[3] indicated that slightly less than half of the cases are diagnosed between 13 and 15 weeks of age, and an equal amount spread out between 15 and 24 weeks of age. This first half is at approximately the age at which distemper and hepatitis vaccines are given to most dogs. In that study, twice as many males were afflicted as females. It has been shown that females are generally more able to handle stress.[6]

Clinical Signs

A description of symptoms should be prefaced by the warning that any one or several can be evident in other diseases as well,

---

** The numbers in chapter 17 refer to the references listed at the end of the chapter.

and either some or all can be present in the disorder discussed here.

In addition to the foregoing example, HOD's symptoms may include a swelling at the hock joint (see Fig.17-3), loss of appetite, pain in the jaws, a clear discharge at the eyes, bowing of the foreleg below the elbow, and turned-out ("east-west") feet. Fever might not be manifest in the early stages of the disease. Usually there is severe pain in the lower area of the leg, where either the pastern or the hock begins. This typically gives anything from a stiff gait to slight or severe lameness, and the dog may refuse to stand up. Extremely adducted pasterns, described often as soft or "down" are most characteristic of hypertrophic osteodystrophy. Diarrhea often, not always, precedes the episodes by a couple of days to a couple of weeks.

Fig. 17-1. Swollen forelegs at the carpal joints and swollen hock joints, along with splayed front feet and turned-out, weak pasterns are indicative of HOD in the young pup.

Hematological and Histological Indications

A higher than normal level of white blood cells is often an indication of the presence of a viral or bacterial agent, and in HOD there is sometimes a high leukocyte count in bone as well as in the blood. Blood tests can show mytosis, an increase in a certain type of leukocyte, and anemia to a slight degree is usually found. Chemical analysis discovers low serum ascorbic acid (Vitamin C).

Radiographic Signs

Correct diagnosis is best made by X-ray film examination along with observation of clinical signs. As young leg bones grow, the end sections are continually changing in composition between cartilage and bone. A short distance from the end, in the metaphyseal region, is a transverse line of cells known as a growth plate. In order to make the bone increase in length, cartilage near the end of the shaft is replaced by bone cells while bone cells in the epiphysis are transformed to cartilage at the growth plate. Meanwhile, cartilage on the far end of the epiphysis ossifies and is itself added to by simple cell division growth.[10] The greatest change occurs in the distal end of the lower leg, where growth is apparently most rapid.

When HOD strikes, the metaphysis becomes generally more dense and thus more opaque to X-rays, and usually becomes

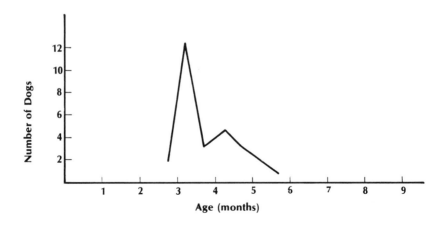

Fig. 17-2. Age distribution.

somewhat more enlarged (it is normally wider in the growing dog, in proportion to the shaft, than it is in the adult) (see Figs. 17-4 a and b). The epiphysis and growth plate largely retain a normal appearance, but parallel to the growth plate a short distance into the metaphysis a radiolucent line appears.[11] It is quite noticeable in the increased-radiodense end of the metaphysis closest to the growth plate. Sometimes the opaque appearance is irregular, granular, and discontinuous, which some investigators in the 1960's felt to be an indication of either a separate disease or a variant of HOD called osteodystrophy-II.[13] As the disorder advances, or in dogs suffering from a more severe form or phase, there often is an enlargement of the end of the ulna above the epiphysis, and bony (calcium) deposits form on the outside of the periosteum, preceded or accompanied by hemorrhage beneath as well as outside the periosteum, and blood cell infiltration into the bone itself.

The periosteum is the tough, smooth, elastic, white covering of bones, and it serves as a point of attachment for other connective tissues such as ligaments, cartilage, and the fascia of muscles.

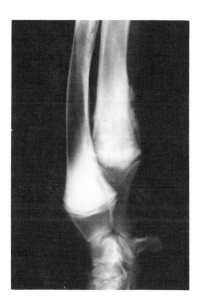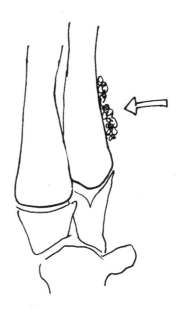

Fig. 17-3. Four month old Great Dane with generalized radiographic evidence of HOD associated with all limbs including epiphyses. (Note bony growth on outside of periosteum of ulna in the metaphyseal area.)

Radiograph compliments of Professor Jan E. Bartels, D.V.M., M.S., Auburn University School of Veterinary Medicine.

The ossification shows up on the radiograph as a billowy or beaded opaque deposit separated from the metaphysis by a translucent line at the periosteum (see Fig.17-3). The swelling resulting from such hemorrhage and bony growths is often very warm and always painful. Such deposits are not usually found in areas of slower growth such as the proximal metaphysis of the radius and ulna, but can be quite massive on the distal end in just a couple of weeks after symptoms commence. As the disease runs its course and the patient recovers, the mineralization outside the periosteum is gradually resorbed and the radiographic appearance of the metaphysis resumes normal shape and density. At the same time, body temperature has returned to normal, lameness begins to subside, and appetite returns.

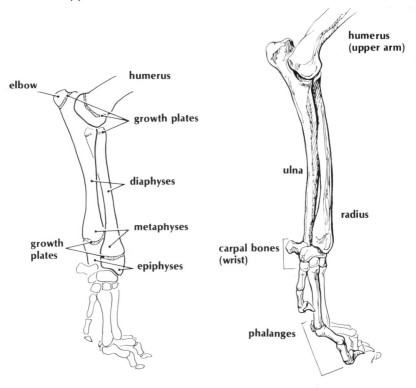

Fig. 17-4 (a). The growing pup. Note that ends of limbs are not yet fused to the shafts, and are wider, or of greater diameter.
(b) Radius and ulna of adult dog, showing closed growth plates with epiphysis united with metaphysis. Ends of the shaft are now more like the centers in diameter.

Treatment

By 1957 it was obvious[9] that Vitamin D increase was not effective, and in the mid-sixties breeders were warned against "mineral overloading" (calcium supplements in the diet).[13] Yet even in the present decade, calcium has been prescribed for HOD! Vitamin C therapy gained the most proponents because serum ascorbic acid analysis showed minimally to considerably low Vitamin C in the blood. However, large doses failed to give consistent results. Researchers at Cornell[16] claimed the studies supporting the use of Vitamin C were uncontrolled and the results equivocal. Some dogs had a temporary remission, others were totally unaffected. Penicillin, streptomycin, sulfa, and other antibiotics have been administered with no reliable beneficial results. As in the case of panosteitis,[8] it appears that the dog will get better whether or not it is treated at all, and regardless of diet except for the harmful addition of calcium and Vitamin D.

This is not to say the disorder is inconsequential. Indeed, breeders have lost some very promising show prospect puppies, and pups intended for family pets have also succumbed to HOD. The fatality rate is too erratic to reliably measure. In some reports it has been 25-35 percent[5,17] and in others it was under four percent.[3] In every case, it is traumatic because of the pup's pain and the owner's helplessness and frustration. At present, the only generally recognized treatment prescribed is symptomatic—relief of pain through buffered aspirin or sometimes corticosteroids.

Similar Diseases

Panosteitis[8] usually occurs in older dogs more than does HOD, and is less severe with a zero fatality risk in itself. Moeller-Barlow's Disease[3] has less fever associated with it according to some reports[9] but others believe it to be the same lesion. HOD resembles scurvy in humans,[17] and radiology shows features of both clinical rickets and scurvy. Osteodystrophy-II is probably not a separate problem, but is a stage in the progression of HOD, beyond which some individuals never go before recovering. Hypertrophic pulmonary osteoarthropathy[2] also has periosteal new bone formation at the distal ends of the extremities, but is almost always accompanied by lung diseases and the osteophytes are more in the wrist and hock than in the long bones. Legg-Calve-Perthe's disease[2] and hip dysplasia[7] involve the proximal end of the femur. Osteochondritis dissecans of the shoulder and knee

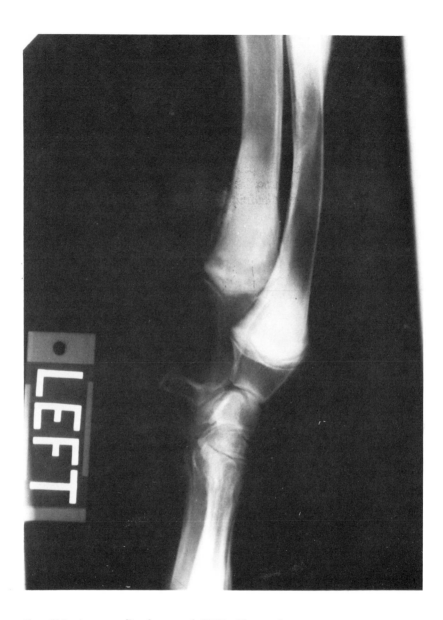

Fig. 17-5. A generalized case of HOD. The patient was a four-month old Great Dane puppy with radiographic changes associated with all limbs and epiphyses.

Radiograph compliments Professor Jan. E. Bartels, D.V.M., M.S., Auburn University School of Veterinary Medicine.

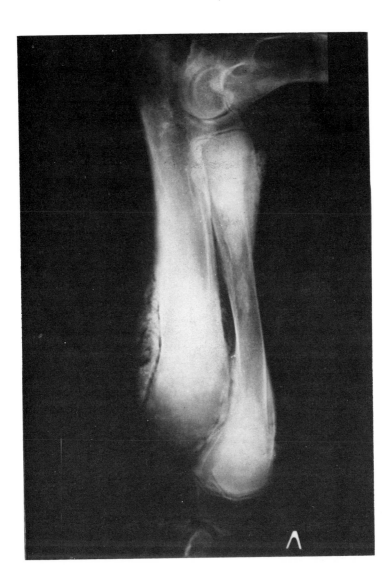

Fig. 17-6. A 4½ month old Great Dane suffering from HOD. It was treated with antibiotics, prednisolone, ascorbic acid, multivitamins and large doses of Vitamin D. The radiograph shows much calcium deposited outside the periosteum of both the radius and ulna. This was the only dog in the 1971-74 Norwegian study which developed "classical" hypertrophy.

Courtesy Dr. Jorann Grondalen,
Norges Veterinarhogskole, Oslo, Norway

(stifle) and some elbow disorders can give similar clinical signs, [10] but are readily identifiable radiographically.

Cause

The cause of HOD is unknown. This is the message that comes out of all the work done so far, and the picture is unlikely to get any better until there is sufficient information and controlled studies to yield some scientific conclusions. One veterinarian/breeder published in the newsletter of the Irish Setter Club of America a questionnaire, [18] in which he sought answers to some 32 questions designed to uncover a connection with another disease, diet, or genetics. Almost no one respnded, [20] although Irish Setter publications had carried a number of tear-jerking case histories and warnings about HOD. [19] Apathy will certainly hinder the fight.

Perhaps some group will find the interest and the contributions, and fund sufficient research to solve the HOD enigma. I know of at least one team of radiologists and immunologists ready to go to work under such a grant.

Infectious agent as a cause?

I believe there is enough evidence to suspect a viral agent at the heart of hypertrophic osteodystrophy, and have found some measure of agreement in the veterinary profession. A familial relationship could easily be suspected when in reality physical contact, proximity, or a carrier might well be the chief factor in the transmission of HOD. Most cases are diagnosed at approximately the age at which distemper vaccine (at least, the "adult" shots) is administered, and many have shown initial symptoms one to six weeks after vaccination. [3] The fact that fever accompanies other signs, and the additional history of diarrhea frequently preceding the onset of pain are indications that a virus or bacteria could be the causative agent. In humans, measles virus has caused bone disease surprisingly similar to canine HOD. [12] Nearly every dog fancier knows of the similarity between measles and distemper viruses, the former being used in a modified version to immunize very young puppies against distemper before the pups are completely weaned. Incidentally, there is some suspicion that human multiple sclerosis is related to canine distemper virus, [1] though it is an unproven theory as yet.

An attempt to induce HOD in healthy dogs by transferring the disease from affected dogs was planned in Norway [3] and partially completed, but with somewhat disappointing results. Blood was transfused from a dog in the acute stage of HOD to healthy dogs of different breeds, and some developed distemper and died! Their blood donor had been vaccinated against distemper and hepatitis one week before it showed signs of HOD. Other dogs died after receiving blood from another HOD-affected donor, but none of the recipients developed signs of HOD. Interestingly, there was an epidemic of distemper in the area at the time, but less than three years after that HOD had almost disappeared, with only two dogs being diagnosed for it since the 26 cases at the clinic in 1976. Could there be an immunizing effect by distemper virus? Could HOD transmitted in blood cause distemper?

Diet

The effect of diet as a causative factor is equivocal, but there is no doubt that excessive calcium supplementation can greatly exacerbate the pain and radiographic signs. As a general rule, stay away from calcium/vitamin D additions to the food since it not only makes HOD worse, it contributes to the severity of other orthopedic and systemic disorders as well. Even ad libitum feeding of high-nutrient density, balanced dog food without extra calcium has resulted in experimentally induced HOD.[4,16] If a growing dog eats all it wants of a "good" dog food, it can absorb more calcium than is beneficial compared to a pup on a restricted diet. Keep your puppies on the thin side, and you can avoid some health problems.

Vitamin C

The great Vitamin C controversy is far from over. Man has apparently benefitted from very large doses during times when the body is under stress as a result of viral and other infections, but most animals make their own ascorbate (Vitamin C). Newborn puppies synthesize their own even when the colostrum and bitch milk have elevated Vitamin C levels, and relatively large doses of the vitamin sometimes have little effect on either the production rate of self-synthesized serum ascorbate or on the course of certain diseases such as HOD, hepatitis,[16] kennel cough, etc. But Vitamin C proponents usually claim the doses were not large enough. There is considerable agreement that stress lowers the ascorbate level in the blood, and that levels are lower in HOD dogs, hence the advocacy of megavitamin-C therapy for HOD. It will be worthwhile to check it out thoroughly.[6]

Conclusions

Hypertrophic Osteodystrophy, or Metaphyseal Osteopathy, is an orthopedic disease in medium, large, and giant breeds, more common in some than in others. There may be several causative factors including heredity, infection, and diet, but it appears to this writer that an infectious agent is the most likely culprit, with calcium supplementation or unlimited feeding of pups resulting in mineral overloading as an intensifier of pain and abnormal bone growth. Some dogs may be more genetically predisposed to HOD, especially fast-growing large breeds.

As in the case of panosteitis, the disease appears to be both self-limited and independent of treatment. Although there are some deaths, probably due to "complications," most pups out-grow HOD within anywhere from one week to several months. Multiple relapses are common, and the same bones can be affected more than once. Extraperiosteal calcification is slowly resorbed and radiodensity of the affected limbs returns to normal. Some individuals are left with permanently bowed forelegs because the ulna has grown at a different rate than the radius, and some are cowhocked for life. Most, however, endure and survive the effects of HOD without permanent damage.

References for Chapter 17

1. Cook, S.D., reported in Nourse, A.E. column: *Family Doctor:* Good Housekeeping Magazine, Oct. 1979.

2. Ettinger, S.J. (editor): *Textbook of Veterinary Internal Medicine,* Vol. 2 (Saunders, Phila., 1975).

3. Grondalen, J.: *Metaphyseal Osteopathy (Hypertrophic Osteo-dystrophy) in Growing Dogs. A Clinical Study.* J. Small Anim. Pract. 17:721-735, (1976). Also, a letter to the editor, same journal, Oct. 1978.

4. Hedhammar, A., et al: *Overnutrition and Skeletal Disease.* Cornell Vet. Vol 64, suppl. 5 (April, 1974).

5. Holmes, J.R.: *Suspected Skeletal Scurvy in the Dog.* Vet Rec. 74:801 (1962).

6. Kronfeld, D.S.: *Home Cooking for Dogs,* Part IX. Pure-Bred Dogs/American Kennel Gazette, pp. 50-52 (Nov., 1978).

7. Lanting, F.L.: *Hip Dysplasia* (ms in press, also series in Dog World, beginning Sept. 1978).

8. Lanting, F.L. *Panosteitis.* Pure-Bred Dogs/American Kennel Gazette (May, 1979).

9. Meier, H., et al: *Hypertrophic Osteodystrophy Associated With Disturbance of Vitamin C Synthesis in Dogs.* J. Am. Vet. Med. Assoc. 130:483 (1957).

10. Olsson, S.-E.: *Osteochondrosis - A Growing Problem to Dog Breeders.* Gaines Progress, Summer 1976, Gaines Dog Research Center.

11. Olsson, S.-E.: *Radiology in Veterinary Pathology.* Acta. Radiol., Suppl. 319, pp. 255-270 (Stockholm, 1972).

12. Pechman, R. Jr.: personal communication, Auburn University, 1979.

13. Riser, W.H.: *Radiographic Differential Diagnosis of Skeletal Diseases of Young Dogs.* J. Am. Vet Radiol. Soc. 5:26 (1964).

14. Riser, W.H. and Miller, H.: *Canine Hip Dysplasia and How to Control It.* (OFA and Hip Dysplasia Control Registry, Phila., 1966).

15. Riser, W.H. and Shirer, J.F.: *Normal and Abnormal Growth of the Distal Foreleg in Large and Giant Dogs.* J. Am. Vet Radiol. Soc., 6:50-64 (1965).

16. Sheffey, B.E., et al: *Vitamin C in the Nutrition of Dogs.* Cornell Vet. 1978.

17. Watson, A.D.J., et al: *Hypertrophic Osteodystrophy in the Dog.* Australian Vet. Jrnl., 49:433-439 (Sept., 1973).

18. Wright, R.P.: Questionnaire on HOD-affected Irish Setters. ISCA "Memo" (June, 1978).

19. Wright, R.P.: *The Vet and the Setter: Hypertrophic Osteodystrophy.* Setter Magazine, Aug.-Sept. 1978, reprinted in Eastern Irish Setter Assoc.'s "Touch O' Blarney," Oct. 1978

20. Wright, R.P.: personal correspondence, Aug. 1979.

APPENDIX

Representative Statistics in Palpation of Pups and Follow-up Radiography

by R. W. Huff, D.V.M.

Author's note: Dr. Richard Huff is a private practitioner with extensive experience in such special interests as canine ophthalmology, hip dysplasia, reproductive physiology, kennel management, and general surgery (see Norden News, Summer 1975) and annually presents numerous seminars and lectures for veterinarians and laymen throughout the United States. This author has worked with Dr. Huff for many years in regard to numerous litters and individuals involved in his breeding program and research into hip dysplasia. This appendix is taken from Dr. Huff's speech in the spring of 1978 to the Veterinary Orthopedic Society meeting at Snowmass, Colorado. The paper was actually presented in his absence by Dr. Huff's associate, Dr. Lance Adams.

Canine Clinical Coxo-femoral Palpation Study From 1968 to 1978

This study is part of my 22 years of experience with canine hip dysplasia. I have been deeply involved with CHD since I was a student in radiology at Michigan State University in 1956 and my internship at Angell Memorial with Dr. Gerry Schnelle. My practice experience has been largely breeder-oriented, involving a high percentage of large and working dogs.

In March of 1968, Dr. John Bardens lit a fire in the veterinary community by publishing his five-year study of the pectineus muscle in relation to hip dysplasia (VM/SAC Vol. 63, No. 3). He developed the palpation technique for prediction of hip dysplasia. He claimed his technique was 85 percent accurate. That year after the A.A.H.A. meeting a few clinicians decided to attempt to duplicate his clinical work. After two years' work with generous breeders, I knew it was a feasible clinical entity to help solve some breeders' fears about the future of their puppies' hips, in the form of a clinical diagnostic aid with predictability. To date I have completely duplicated Dr. Bardens' technique using plane-three general anesthesia on seven to ten week old puppies. I have tattooed all pups and, to maintain a controlled clinical experiment, have not performed pectineus muscle surgery on any of those palpated.

My philosophy has been to recommend that normal, near-normal and Grade 1 predictions be selected for possible show, working, or breeding animals depending on the outcome of development, gait and motion ability, and radiographs at 24 months of age. Puppies palpated as Grades 2 or 3 were recommended as pets or for future culling or surgery. And, most commonly, Grade 4's were euthanized by most objective breeders. This philosophy has proven to be a great help to breeders and myself as a clinician in promoting canines with stronger pelvic joints and helping pet owners with the future possibilities relative to the CHD problem. As a result I have a large practice of working and companion animals that are sound in the rear quarter at ages over six years compared to the late 1950's and early 1960's when so many animals were euthanized due to crippling CHD.

Following is a chart of 682 consecutive hip palpations done between 1970 and 1976 (out of a total of more than 2500 palpations I have performed), these including many follow-up radiographs and other histories. My definition, used here, of an accurate result was that the follow-up (adult radiograph) history was within one grade as predicted at seven to ten weeks, or that the animal had a pectineus myectomy performed at six months or older due to gross pain and/or lameness when the prediction was Grade 1 or worse. Also, animals euthanized after six months due to lameness were radiographed at that time and results sent to me. An innaccurate result was tabulated by a 24-month radiograph that was more than one grade off in either direction. Dr. Schnelle's standard grading system of normal and near-normal, Grades 1, 2, 3, and 4, has been used consistently for 20 years in my practice.

I feel competent in the use of the Bardens technique as a clinical diagnostic aid in my programs for both breeders and pet owners. It certainly has eliminated a great deal of "man's fear of the unknown" and helped many to make early decisions about puppies.

TABLE 1. ACCURACY OF PALPATION vs. X-RAYS.

Breed	Number Palpated	X-rayed or Reported Back	Accurate Result	Inaccurate Result
German Shepherd Dog	327	119	108	11
Saint Bernard	32	11	10	1
Irish Setter	8	8	8	
German Wire-haired Pointer	5	3	3	
Golden Retriever	113	25	18	7
Old English Sheepdog	119	39	35	4
Newfoundland	45	31	30	1
Elkhound	2			
Afghan Hound	2			
Great Dane	1			
Giant Schnauzer	1			
Labrador Retriever	2			
Bloodhound	24	11	11	
German Short-haired Pointer	1	1	1	
Totals	682	248	224	24

With a 35 percent follow-up during this most accurate time (earlier results may be colored by the learning process and later palpations had no two-year radiographs to compare), we see 90 percent accurate results.

There are seven factors that I use today before giving my personal certification of an animal as free of dysplasia:

1. Parents' and other relatives' histories with radiographs;

2. Palpation at seven to ten weeks of age;

3. Soundness during pediatric period (4 to 11 months of age);

4. Nutritional level, especially overfeeding of carbohydrates during pediatric period, proper exercise, pelvic injuries;

5. Normal radiograph at 12 months or older depending upon size of breed, plus a normal gait and motion analysis;

6. Test breeding and progeny palpation; and

7. Finally, a 24- to 36-month normal radiograph, depending on size of breed and complete maturity.

I feel certain that we are dealing with a polygenic heredity/environment problem that can never be eliminated but *can* be diluted to a minimal level. If we stay open-minded and objective, and are willing to change as newer theories come along, the future of this major clinical problem is bright for the veterinarian and the dog-owning public.

References

1. Bado, J.L.: *Etiology and Treatment of Congenital Dysplasia of the Hip.* (abstract) J. Bone & Jt. Surg. *43A*:287 (March, 1961).

2. Bardens, J.W.: personal communication (1976).

3. Bardens, J.W.: Palpation for the Detection of Dysplasia and Wedge Technique for Pelvic Radiography. Proc. 39th Annu. Meet. AAHA, Las Vegas, Nev. pp. 468-471 (1972).

4. Bardens, J.W.: *Palpation for the Detection of Joint Laxity.* Proc. OFA Symp., St. Louis, Mo. (1972).

5. Bardens, J.W.: *Hip Dysplasia, a Biomechanical Disease.* unpublished script of speech to veterinary conference, Fiji Is. (1975).

6. Bardnes, J.W.: *Joint Laxity as Hip Dysplasia.* Proc. OFA Symp., St. Louis, Mo. (1972).

7. Bardens, J.W.: *Breeding Control Program for Normal Hips.* unpublished script of speech to veterinary conference, Fiji Is. (1975).

8. Bardens, J.W. and Hardwick, H.: *New Observations on the Diagnosis and Cause of Hip Dysplasia.* Vet. Med./Small Anim. Clin., *63*:238-245 (1968).

9. Belfield, W.O.: *Chronic Subclinical Scurvy and Canine Hip Dysplasia.* Vet. Med./Small Anim. Clin., pp. 1399-1401 (Oct., 1976) plus reprint of same, with comments added by its author, published by him in 1977.

10. Beling, C.G., et al: *Metabolism of Estradiol in Greyhounds and German Shepherd Dogs.* Acta Radiol., Suppl. 344, p. 109 (1975).

11. Bornfors, S.: Palsson, K.: and Skude, G.: *Hereditary Aspects of Hip Dysplasia in German Shepherd Dogs.* J. Am. Vet. Med. Assoc. *145*:15-20 (1964).

202

12. Brookes, M. and Wardle, E.N.: *Muscle Action and Shape of the Femur.* J. Bone & Jt. Surg. *44B*:398-411 (May, 1962).

13. Burton, A.R.C.: *Scurvy in the Anarctic.* Lancet, pp. 1146-1147 (1972).

14. Cardinet, G.H. III; Guffy, M.M.; Wallace, L.J.: *Canine Hip Dysplasia: Effects of Pectineal Tenotomy on the Coxofemoral Joints of German Shepherd Dogs.* J. Am. Vet. Med. Assoc. *164* (March 15, 1974).

15. Cardinet, G.H.; Wallace, L.J.; Fedde, M.R.; and Guffy, M.M.: *Developmental Myelopathy in the Canine with Type II Muscle Fiber Hypertrophy.* Arch. Neurol. *21*:620-630 (1969).

16. Carlson, W.D.: *Veterinary Radiology.* Lea & Febinger, Philadelphia, Pa. (1967).

17. Corley, E.A.: *Canine Hip Dysplasia and the Orthopedic Foundation for Animals.* OFA brochure, undated, three pages.

18. Crawford, R.D. and Kaye, M.M.: *A Proposed Canadian Selective Registration Scheme for Control of Canine Hip Dysplasia.* Proc. OFA Symp., St. Louis, Mo. (1972).

19. Due, J.: notice re "a" stamp in advertising, The German Shepherd Dog Review, published by GSDC of America, p. 104 (Jan., 1979).

20. Edqvist, L.E., et. al: *Blood Plasma Levels of Progesterone and Oestradiol in the Dog During Oestrus Cycle and Pregnancy.* Acta Endocrin. *78*:554 (1975).

21. Engel, W.K. and Karpati, G.: *Impaired Skeletal Muscle Maturation Following Neonatal Neuectomy.* Devel. Biol. *17*:713-723 (June, 1968).

22. Faulkner, L.C.: *What Are We Doing About the Pet Population Problem?* speech, Morris Animal Foundation seminar, Los Angeles, Calif. (April 21, 1973).

23. Giardina, J.F.: *The SV "a" Stamp vs. the OFA Certification.* German Shepherd Dog Review (October, 1976).

24. Giardina, J.F. and MacCarthy, A.W.: *Salvaging the Predysplastic Puppy for Use as a Working Dog.* Vet. Med./Small Anim. Clin. *67*(July, 1972).

25. Gustafsson, P.-O.: *Hip Dysplasia in the Greyhound.* J. Am. Vet. Radiol. Soc. *9*:47 (1968).

26. Gustafsson, P.-O., et al: *Growth and Remodeling of the Hip Joint.* Acta Radiol., Suppl. 319 (1972).

27. Gustafsson, P.-O, et al: *Growth and Mitiotic Rate of the Proximal Tibial Epiphyseal Plate in Hypophysectomized Rats Given Estradiol and Human Growth Hormone.* Acta Radiol., Suppl. 344 (1975).

28. Gustafsson, P.-O., et. al: *Skeletal Development of Greyhounds, German Shepherd Dogs, and Their Crossbreed Offspring.* Acta Radiol., Suppl. 344 (1975).

29. Gustafsson, P.-O., et al: *Skeletal Development and Sexual Maturation.* Acta Radiol., Suppl. 319 (1972).

30. Hedhammar, A., et al: *Overnutrition and Skeletal Disease.* Cornell Vet. Vol. 64, Suppl. 5 (April, 1974).

31. Henricson, B.; Norberg, I.; and Olsson, S.-E.: *On the Etiology and Pathogenesis of Hip Dysplasia: A Comparative Review.* J. Small Anim. Pract. 7:673-688 (Nov., 1966).

32. Henricson, B., et al: *Hip Dysplasia in Sweden: Controlled Breeding Programs.* Proc. OFA Symp., St. Louis, Mo. (1972).

33. Henry, J.D. Jr. and Park, R.D.: *Wedge Technique for Demonstration of Coxofemoral Joint Laxity in the Canine.* Proc. OFA Symp., St. Louis, Mo. (1972).

34. Humane Society of U.S.: *The Pet Population Explosion.* brochure, undated, HSUS, 1604 K St. N.W., Washington, D.C. 20006.

35. Hutt, F.B.: *Genetic Selection to Reduce the Incidence of Hip Dysplasia in Dogs.* J. Am. Vet. Med. Assoc. 151:1041-1048 (1967).

36. Jessen, C.R. and Spurrell, F.A.: *Radiographic Detection of Canine Hip Dysplasia in Known Age Groups.* Proc. OFA Symp., St. Louis, Mo. (1972).

37. Kaman, C.H. and Gossling, H.R.: *A Breeding Program to Reduce Hip Dysplasia in German Shepherd Dogs.* J. Am. Vet. Med. Assoc. 151:562-571 (Sept. 1, 1967).

38. Kaman, C.H. and Gossling, H.R.: *Report on Some Breeding Aspects of Hip Dysplasia.* Dog World (Nov., 1967).

39. Kasstrom, H.: *Nutrition, Weight Gain, and Development of Hip Dysplasia.* Acta Radiol., Suppl. 344 (1975).

40. Kasstrom, H.: *Estrogens, Nutrition, and Hip Dysplasia in the Dog.* Dept. of Clinical Radiology, Royal Veterinary College, Stockholm, Sweden (1975).

41. Kasstrom, H., et al: *Growth and Remodeling of the Hip Joint and Proximal Femur in Adolescent Dogs.* Acta Radiol., Suppl. 344 (1975).

42. Kasstrom, H., et al: *Plasma Levels of Estradiol and Plasma Protein Binding of Sex Steroids in Dogs.* Acta Radiol., Suppl. 344 (1975).

43. Kronfeld, D.S.: *Home Cooking for Dogs,* Part IX. Pure-Bred Dogs/American Kennel Gazette, pp. 52-53 (Nov., 1978).

44. Lanting, F.L. and Bardens, J.W.: Interview. German Shepherd Dog Review (July through December, 1978).

45. Lanting, F.L.: *Hip Dysplasia* (series), Dog World (beginning with Sept., 1978 issue).

46. Larsen, J.S.: *Prevalence of Hip Dysplasia According to Radiographic Evaluations Among 36 Breeds of Dogs.* Proc. OFA Symp., St. Louis, Mo. (1972).

47. Lewis, D.G.: letter to the editor, The Veterinary Record. p. 69 (Jan. 21, 1978).

48. Lust, G.; Geary, J.C.; and Sheffey, B.E.; *Development of Hip Dysplasia in Dogs.* Am. J. Vet. Res., Vol. 34 (1973).

49. Lust, G.: *Hip Dysplasia in Dogs: Its Heritable Nature.* Cornell Research Lab Report, Series 2, Number 8 (June, 1977).

50. Lust, G. and Farrell, P.W.: *Hip Dysplasia in Dogs: The Interplay of Genotype and Environment.* Cornell Vet., Vol. 67 (Oct., 1977).

51. Lust, G., et al: *Changes in Pelvic Muscle Tissue Associated with Hip Dysplasia in Dogs.* Am. J. Vet. Res. 33:1097-1108 (1972).

52. Lust, G., et al: *Studies on Pectineus Muscle in Canine Hip Dysplasia.* Cornell Vet. 62:628-645 (1972).

53. McClave, P.L.: *Elimination of Coxofemoral Dysplasia from a Breeding Kennel.* Vet. Med. 52:241-243 (May, 1957).

54. Mansson, J. and Norberg, I.: *Dysplasia of the Hip in Dogs.* Medical Bulletin of the Sveriges Vetrinarforbund 13:330-339 (1961).

55. Morgan, J.P.: *Radiographic Diagnosis of Hip Dysplasia in Skeletally Mature Dogs.* Proc. OFA Symp., St. Louis, Mo. (1972).

56. NRC Committee on Animal Nutrition: *Nutrient Requirements of Dogs.* National Acad. of Sci., National Research Council. Number 8. Washington, D.C. (1972).

57. Olsson, S.-E.: *What To Do About Hip Dysplasia.* German Shepherd Dog Review (Feb., 1976).

58. Olsson, S.-E.: *What to Do About Hip Dysplasia:* Pure-Bred Dogs/American Kennel Gazette (August, 1974).

59. Olsson, S.-E.: *The Control of Hip Dysplasia in the Scandinavian Countries.* Small Anim. Pract. 3:112-116 (1962).

60. Olsson, S.-E. and Kasstrom, H.: *Etiology and Pathogenesis of Canine Hip Dysplasia.* Proc. OFA Symp., St. Louis, Mo. (1972).

61. Orr, N.W.M.: *Sled Dogs in the Antarctic.* Brit. J. Nutr., Vol. 20 (1966).

62. Patterson, D.F.: *New Developments in Canine Medical Genetics.* Pure-Bred Dogs/American Kennel Gazette (Oct., 1975).

63. Payne, P.R., in Graham-Jones: *Canine and Feline Nutritional Requirements.* pp. 19-31. Pergamon Press, Oxford, England. (1965).

64. Pierce, K.R.: Bridges, C.H.; and Banks, W.C.: *Hormone-induced Hip Dysplasia in Dogs.* J. Small Anim. Pract. 6:121-126 (1965).

65. Priester, W.A. and Mulvihill, J.J.: *Canine Hip Dysplasia: Relative Risk by Sex, Size, and Breed, and Comparative Aspects.* J. Am. Vet. Med. Assoc. 160:735-739 (March 1, 1972).

66. Riser, W.H.: *Canine Hip Dysplasia: Cause and Control.* J. Am. Vet. Med. Assoc. 165:360-362 (Aug. 15, 1974).

67. Riser, W.H.: *A New Look at Developmental Subluxation and Dislocation: Hip Dysplasia in the Dog.* J. Small Anim. Pract. 4:421-434 (Dec., 1963).

68. Riser, W.H.: personal communication. (Feb. & Oct., 1978).

69. Riser, W.H.: *Growth and Development of the Normal Canine Pelvic, Hip Joints, and Femurs from Birth to Maturity:* A Radiographic Study. J. Am. Vet. Radiol. Soc. 14:24-34 (1973).

70. Riser, W.H.: *The Dog as a Model for the Study of Hip Dysplasia.* Vet. Path. 12, Number 4:233-334 (1975).

71. Riser, W.H. and Miller, H.: *Canine Hip Dysplasia and How to Control It.* OFA and ip Dysplasia Control Registry, Philadelphia, Pa. (1966).

72. Riser, W.H. and Shirer, J.F.: *Hip Dysplasia: Coxofemoral Abnormalities in Neonatal German Shepherd Dogs.* J. Small Anim. Pract. 7:7-12 (1966).

73. Riser, W.H. and Shirer, J.F.: *Correlation Between Canine Hip Dysplasia and Pelvic Muscle Mass, a Study of 95 Dogs.* Am. J. Vet. Res. 28:769-777 (1967).

74. Riser, W.H., et al: *Influence of Early Rapid Growth and Weight Gain on Hip Dysplasia in the German Shepherd Dog.* J. Am. Vet Med. Assoc. 145:661-668(1964).

75. Samuelson, M.L.: *Correlation of Palpation with Radiography in Diagnosis and Prognosis of Canine Hip Dysplasia.* Proc. OFA Symp., St. Louis, Mo. (1972).

76. Schales, O.: *Genetic Aspects of Dysplasia of the Hip Joint.* N. AM. Vet. 37 (1956).

77. Schnelle, G.B.: letter to editor. German Shepherd Dog Review, p. 88 (Jan., 1976).

78. Schnelle, G.B.: *Thoughts on Hip Dysplasia.* Proc. OFA Symp., St. Louis, Mo. (1972).

79. Schnelle, G.B.: letter to editor. J. Am. Vet. Med. Assoc. (Aug. 1, 1972).

80. Schnelle, G.B.: *The Present Status and Outlook on Canine Hip Dysplasia.* Gaines Progress (Spring, 1973).

81. Schnelle, G.B.: *Some New Diseases in the Dog.* American Kennel Gazette Vol. 52 (1935).

82. Schnelle, G.B.: *Congenital Dysplasia of the Hip.* Proc. 91st Annu. Meet., Am. Vet. Med. Assoc. pp. 253-258 (1954).

83. Stone, I.: *The Healing Factor.* Grosset & Dunlap, New York, N.Y. (1972).

84. Thomas, L.: *Medicine in America.* TV Guide (Dec. 31, 1977).

85. Trueta, J.: *Skeletal Shape and Muscle Power.* Bulletin Hosp. Bone Dis. (Oct., 1960).

86. Trueta, J.: *Studies of the Development and Decay of the Human Frame,* Saunders, Philadelphia, Pa. (1968).

87. von Stephanitz, M.: *The German Shepherd Dog,* 8th Edition. Verein fur Deutsche Schaferhunde, Augsburg, Germany (1932).

88. Whittington, K., et al: *Report of the Panel on Canine Hip Dysplasia.* J. Am. Vet. Med. Assoc. 139:791:806 (Oct. 1, 1961).

About the Author

Fred L. Lanting has been involved with purebred dogs since 1945 and has been actively breeding German Shepherd Dogs since 1967. In the same year he began handling and became an all-breed professional handler by 1978, giving up handling in 1979 to become an AKC provisional judge. In the course of these 13 years Mr. Lanting has also researched and worked with the leading specialists in the field of canine orthopedics, and has become known as the leading non-veterinarian authority on canine hip dysplasia in the United States today. Through this research Lanting has applied his knowledge to the art and practice of breedings dogs and is now producing litters with a consistently and extremely high percentage of normal hips.

Fred graduated from West Virginia Wesleyan College in 1957 with a B.S. in chemistry and pre-veterinary studies. His post graduate studies include chemistry, physics, and education. He has worked in a community college in New Jersey as head of the Science Department and also as a research and development chemist. He is currently employed as a Senior Technical Representative for the Plastics Division of Diamond Shamrock Corporation.

Multi-talented, Lanting has also published two works of poetry, *Translation*, and *Forms and Shadows*. His articles on dogs have appeared in *Pure-Bred Dogs/American Kennel Gazette*, the *German Shepherd Dog Club of America Review*, *Dog World*, and *Dogs in Canada*. He is a member of the German Shepherd Dog Club of America and has held various offices in all-breed and German Shepherd Dog clubs throughout the country.

Fred and wife reside in Union Grove, Alabama, where he continues limited breeding of German Shepherd Dogs and pursues his interest in writing about the canine maladies which concern us today.

Index

AN AFTERTHOUGHT

I need not read into your eyes
Anthropomorphic fantasies,
Nor mysteries
Of ancient Eastern rite,
As some with Siamese or Persians might.
Your love's an open book:
You look
To me as I to Paradise.
My finger traces "dog" on frosted glass
And you, from out there on the grass,
Perceive me writing "god."

FLL